lonely planet

POCKET
PORTLAND
& THE WILLAMETTE VALLEY

Brett Atkinson & Margot Bigg

Contents

Top: Food carts in Downtown Portland
Bottom: The Columbia River Gorge

Plan Your Trip 4

The Journey Begins Here 4
Our Picks 6
Perfect Days 24
Get Prepared 28
When To Go 30
Getting There 32
Getting Around 33
A Few Surprises 36

Explore Portland 38

Downtown & Southwest Portland 41
Washington Park 54
Old Town Chinatown 59
Northwest Portland & Pearl District 73
Northeast & North Portland 89
Southeast Portland 103
McMinnville 127
Newberg & Dundee 139
Salem 149

Portland Toolkit 160

Family Travel 162
Accommodations 163
Food, Drink & Nightlife 164
LGBTIQ+ Travel 166
Health & Safe Travel 167
Responsible Travel 168
Accessible Travel 170
Nuts & Bolts 171
Index 172

FROM TOP LEFT: HRACH HOVHANNISYAN/SHUTTERSTOCK, WITOLD SKRYPCZAK/ALAMY

★ Top Experiences

Portland Saturday Market 62
Lan Su Chinese Garden 64
Powell's City of Books 76
Forest Park 78
McMenamins Kennedy School 92
Oregon Museum of Science & Industry 106
The Oregon Garden 151
Silver Falls State Park 152
Willamette Valley Wine Touring 129
Wine Touring Around Newberg & Dundee 141

The Journey Begins Here

As a child, when I'd mention I was from Portland, I'd usually have to explain it was 'north of San Francisco.' Nowadays it seems everyone is familiar with Portland, and if they know anything about wine, they know the Willamette Valley, too. While outdoorsy folks have always been aware of Portland's proximity to wild beaches and pristine forests, these days the city is equally known for its culinary scene, and for its quirkiness. Now when I tell people I'm from Portland, they not only know it – they gush about it. *Passage written by Margot Bigg.*

Brett Atkinson

@travelwriternz

New Zealand-based travel, food and beer writer, Brett Atkinson never needs a second invitation to cross the Pacific and explore his favorite American state.

Margot Bigg

@margotbigg

Margot was born and (mostly) raised in Portland. After many years living in India, France and the UK, she once again calls the City of Roses home.

Harvey Milk St, Portland

DAVID BUZZARD/ALAMY

AKES
P
2
65957

THE BEST

Wellness Experiences

Gone are the days when wellness experiences were limited to soaks in forested hot springs. While there's plenty of that to go around, formal spas are growing in popularity across the region.

Soak away your stress in a bath infused with red wine – while sipping on a glass of wine – at the **Wine Spa** (pictured above), a vinotherapy-focused concept spa in Northeast Portland. (p96)

Descend into a subterranean hydrotherapy circuit with soaking tubs and saunas at **Cascada Thermal Springs + Hotel** in the Alberta Arts District. (p96)

Plunge into a heated outdoor pool in a former teacher's lounge at **McMenamins Kennedy School** (pictured above), an old elementary school-turned-hotel and dining complex in a Portland neighborhood. (p92)

Right: Cascada Thermal Springs + Hotel

FROM LEFT: KARA COOPER/THE WINE SPA, KAT NYBERG/MCMENAMINS, CARLA JULIETT/CASCADA

EXIT

THE BEST

Literary Experiences

Rainy days and gray skies don't necessarily keep Oregonians from going outdoors, but they do make the idea of devoting days to reading extra appealing. Fortunately, a good bookstore is never far away.

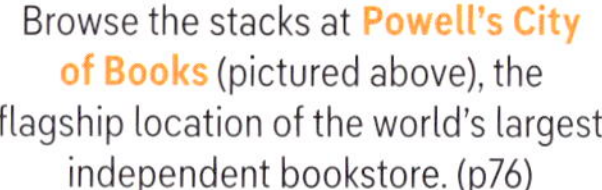

Browse the stacks at **Powell's City of Books** (pictured above), the flagship location of the world's largest independent bookstore. (p76)

Search for rare books about art and architecture or pick up vintage prints at **Monograph Bookwerks** in the Alberta Arts District. (p95)

Pick up books on metaphysical topics or shop for crystals at **New Renaissance Bookstore** in Nob Hill. (p82)

Attend readings and get recommendations on books by Oregon authors at the **Literary Arts Bookstore** in Southeast Portland. (p115)

Stop by **Third Street Books** (pictured above) in McMinnville to check out the massive selection of new and used books. (p133)

Right: Powell's City of Books

FROM LEFT: NCBPHOTOGRAPHY-NANCYCAROL/SHUTTERSTOCK, VISIT MCMINNVILLE, 1000PHOTOGRAPHY/SHUTTERSTOCK

AIRPLANES
MASKS
ORIGAMI

THE BEST

Wine Experiences

If you've heard of the Willamette Valley, the chances that you have a penchant for pinot are high. While Portland has some great wineries in the city, an estate tasting in the countryside is never a bad idea.

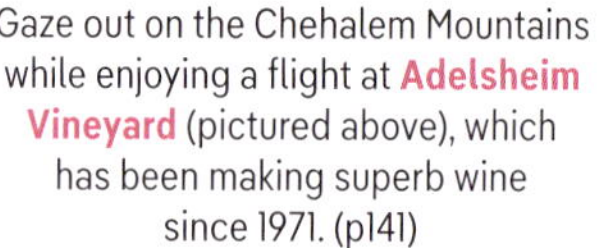

Gaze out on the Chehalem Mountains while enjoying a flight at **Adelsheim Vineyard** (pictured above), which has been making superb wine since 1971. (p141)

Visit Newberg's **Roco Winery** to sample bubbly wines made in the traditional method (aka *méthode champenoise*) using Oregon fruit. (p141)

Try a flight at **Boedecker Cellars** (pictured above), a family-owned-and-operated winery in Northwest Portland with an indoor-outdoor tasting room and great pinot and chardonnay. (p84)

Head to the Dundee Hills to visit the scenic tasting room at **Ambar Estate**, which features Japanese gardens and a fantastic five-course dinner and pairing program. (p142)

Right: Boedecker Cellars

FROM LEFT: JORGE GARRIDO/ALAMY, JAI SOOTS/BOEDECKER CELLARS, SIN SENGMANYPHET/BOEDECKER CELLARS

BOEDECKER
Cellars

THE BEST

Culinary Experiences

Portland has a dining scene to rival those of much bigger cities (which checks out; it is James Beard's hometown, after all). The Willamette Valley wine country isn't far behind.

Feast on a 'botanical tasting menu' that highlights locally foraged and farmed ingredients at **Astera** (pictured above), by chef Aaron Adams. (p168)

Book well in advance for **Kann**, which serves wood-fired Haitian cuisine by star chef Gregory Gourdet. (p112)

Dine on dumplings, bread and more at **Kachka** (pictured above right). (p112)

Savor a multi-course dinner featuring seasonal ingredients at **Langbaan**, a cozy dining experience created by Portland's much-lauded Thai chef, Earl Ninsom. (p85)

Taste what James Beard Award–nominated chef Kari Shaughnessy is up to at McMinnville's **Hayward**, where global influences meet Willamette Valley ingredients. (p136)

Right: Kann

FROM LEFT: JOSHUA CHANG/ASTERA, CARLY DIAZ/KACHKA, STEVE FREIHON/KANN

THE BEST

Bar & Brewery Experiences

With an abundance of microbreweries, cideries, wineries and craft cocktail lounges, you're never far from a good drink in Oregon. With a burgeoning non-alcoholic spirits scene, there's plenty for teetotalers, too.

Sip cider at **Bauman's on Oak** (pictured above), a welcoming family-friendly cidery and pub. (p114)

Head downtown for drinks, DJs and the soothsayers at **Fortune**, a dark lounge inside the Sentinel Hotel. (p51)

Sample cocktails and an extensive food menu at **Victoria Bar**, a popular spot for dining and drinking alike. (p100)

Try cocktails by chef Gregory Gourdet at **Sousòl**, a basement bar below his celebrated restaurant Kann. (p114)

Drink the monk-made Benedict farmhouse ale and St Gabriel Belgian dubbel at the **Benedictine Brewery** in Mt Angel. (p159)

Enjoy **Wilderton Aperitivo Co** (pictured above) tasting room in Hood River while sampling non-alcoholic spirits. (p117)

Right: Cocktail at Sousòl

FROM LEFT: BUZA PHOTOGRAPHY LLC/BAUMAN'S ON OAK, FINN PETERSON/WILDERTON APERITIVO CO, EVA KOSMAS FLORES/SOUSÒL

THE BEST

Shopping Experiences

From gourmet goods made from Oregon-grown ingredients to crafty creations by local makers, there are lots of things that will make you want to part with your cash. Bonus points: there's no sales tax in Oregon.

Spend hours exploring **Cargo** (pictured above), a warehouse showroom where small businesses sell craft supplies, upcycled furniture and ephemera. (p111)

Head to SE Hawthorne St to visit **Gold Door Jewelry & Arts**, which sells imported jewelry and trinkets from Latin America and beyond. (p109)

Browse for vintage apparel and handmade items by local makers at **Alberta Studios**. (p95)

Pick up gifts for the cat-lover in your life at **GiftyKitty**, which stocks cat-themed housewares, jewelry and art, much of it made by local artists. (p101)

Take a gourmet adventure to **Red Hills Market** (pictured above) in Dundee to pick up olive oil, seasonings and other culinary delights. (p145)

Right: GiftyKitty

FROM LEFT: SARAH LYON/CARGO, CANNON PHOTOGRAPHY LLC/ALAMY, CLODY CATES/GIFTYKITTY

THE BEST

Entertainment Experiences

Indie film screenings, comedy shows and theatrical performances will keep you entertained on even the dreariest of evenings. The hard part is figuring out what to choose.

Watch independent films, some by local filmmakers, at **Hollywood Theatre** (pictured above), where the Candyland facade and 70mm projector adds vintage appeal. (p96)

See what's on at Nob Hill's **Cinema 21**, an arthouse theater that screens indie and foreign films. (p83)

Down pizza and frothy beer at the **Kennedy School Theater**, a cozy screening space with sofas inside a schoolhouse-turned-hotel. (p93)

See some of Portland's finest players take the stage at **Portland Center Stage at the Armory**, a Victorian armory transformed into a two-theater performance space. (p83)

Attend a concert or comedy show at Salem's **Elsinore Theatre** (pictured above), a former silent movie theater dating to 1926. (p155)

ANTARES_NS/SHUTTERSTOCK

Bonsai at Lan Su Chinese Garden

THE BEST

Garden Experiences

Portland and the Willamette Valley are lush, with lots of rain and a moderate climate. This climate is ideal for nurturing gorgeous gardens full of flowers, foliage and beautiful trees.

Stroll interconnected pathways and under intricate pavilions amid the **Lan Su Chinese Garden**. (p64)

Meander through a space filled with flowers and foliage at **Crystal Springs Rhododendron Garden**. (p110)

Wander 12 acres of perfectly manicured Japanese-style gardens at **Portland Japanese Garden**. (p54)

Head to Washington Park's **International Rose Test Garden** to take in hundreds of varieties of roses and great city views. (p54)

Explore themed gardens and groves, shop for plants and maybe spot a woodpecker or deer at **Oregon Garden** in Silverton. (p149)

THE BEST

Art Experiences

With exceptional art museums and two different art districts, there's lots for art lovers to see in Portland alone, with more experiences within a day trip's distance away.

Wander the galleries at **Portland Art Museum**, which features a mix of temporary and permanent exhibits, including Indigenous art. (p46)

See the works of budding artists at the **First Thursday Street Gallery**, an outdoor pop-up art space spanning three city blocks. (p81)

Attend gallery openings at **Last Thursday** in the Alberta Arts District. In summer a massive street party is added to the mix. (p97)

Shop for glass ornaments, watch glassblowers at the torch or have a go yourself at **Lincoln City Glass Center** on the Oregon Coast. (p124)

Lincoln City Glass Center

VICTORIA DITKOVSKY/SHUTTERSTOCK

THE BEST

LGBTIQ+ Experiences

Some cities have 'gayborhoods,' but in Portland, the whole city is LGBTIQ+-friendly thanks to an abundance of bars, events and even a bookstore, not to mention plenty of allies.

Watch drag performers take to the stage at **Darcelle XV Showplace**, a Vegas-style cabaret that's been going strong since it first opened back in 1967. (p166)

Party the night away at **Back2Earth**, an inclusive community bar with DJ nights, arcade games and great vibes. (p166)

Browse titles by queer authors, many with LGBTIQ+ themes, at **Always Here Bookstore** in North Portland. (p101)

Celebrate diversity at **Portland Pride Waterfront Festival**, which brings the queer community and allies together every summer. (p30)

Visit Remy Wines in the Dundee Hills to sample wines from community-led wineries at **Queer Wine Fest** (pictured above), the world's first LGBTIQ+ wine festival. (p166)

FROM LEFT: PNG STUDIO PHOTOGRAPHY/SHUTTERSTOCK, ZACHARY GOFF/REMY WINES/QUEER WINE FEST

THE BEST

Outdoor Experiences

Even if you're in the dead center of Portland, you're never far from an outdoor adventure. Hop in your car to get to beaches and waterfalls or simply walk on over to your nearest forest-filled park.

Hike uphill (or up the stairs) to the top of **Mt Tabor Park** (pictured above) for incredible views of Portland. (p110)

Put your legs and lungs to the test by ascending **Saddle Mountain** near the Oregon Coast for clear-day views of the Pacific Ocean. (p123)

See 10 different waterfalls in just a few hours by hiking the 7.2-mile Trail of Ten Falls in **Silver Falls State Park** in the Willamette Valley. (p152)

Experience the enchantment of the woods without leaving the city by taking a hike through **Forest Park**, a 5200-acre park with over 80 miles of walking trails. (p78)

Take a trip to **Multnomah Falls** (pictured above) in the Columbia Gorge – it's the highest waterfall in Oregon. (p117)

Best for Kids

Drop in on **OMSI** (Oregon Museum of Science and Industry), which is equally loved by kids and grownups alike, for its hands-on exhibits, planetarium and military submarine.

Immerse yourself in a high-tech world of lasers and mirrors or hop into an illuminated ball pit at **Hopscotch Portland**.

Appreciate some of the best views of the city from aboard the **Portland Aerial Tram**, just south of downtown.

Make a splash in McMinnville with a visit to the **Evergreen Wings & Waves Waterpark**, a huge indoor complex with slides, wave pools and more.

Take a pony (or a peacock or dragon) for a spin at the **Historic Carousel & Museum** in Albany - a merry-go-round menagerie in the heart of the Willamette Valley.

Best for Free

Browse for handicrafts made by Oregon artisans and listen to live music at the **Portland Saturday Market**.

Flip through a full city block of tomes at **Powell's City of Books** (p76), which claims to be the world's largest new-and-used independent bookstore.

Visit the **Alberta Arts District** (p97) on the last Thursday of the month for gallery openings and, in summer, a vibrant street fair.

Check out whimsical puppets from across the globe at the nonprofit **Portland Puppet Museum**.

Spot up to 10 waterfalls on a 7.2-mile hike along the Trail of Ten Falls in **Silver Falls State Park** (p152), or take a shorter stroll for a taste of the magic.

Perfect Days

Wander through wooded parks and flower-filled gardens, immerse yourself in artistic experiences and eat great meals - perhaps paired with the Willamette Valley's fantastic wine.

Voodoo Doughnut

FROM LEFT: DAVID BUZZARD/SHUTTERSTOCK, B BROWN/SHUTTERSTOCK, HRACH HOVHANNISYAN/SHUTTERSTOCK, DANITA DELIMONT/ALAMY

DAY ONE

Only Have One Day?

MORNING

Start with a visit to **Powell's City of Books** (p76) to beat the crowds before walking to Old Town Chinatown to visit the **Lan Su Chinese Garden** (p64). Grab lunch at one of the eateries at **Pine Street Market** (p70) and dessert at **Voodoo Doughnut** (p67).

AFTERNOON

In the afternoon, take the MAX Light Rail up to **Washington Park** (p54) to visit the **International Rose Test Garden** (p54; pictured above) and the **Portland Japanese Garden** (p54), or go on a stroll through the woods at the **Hoyt Arboretum** (p57).

EVENING

Head to **Cascada Thermal Springs + Hotel** (p96) for a pre-dinner soak, followed by a meal at one of the many restaurants in the **Alberta Arts District** (p97).

DAY TWO

A Weekend Trip

MORNING

Spend your second morning visiting the **Portland Art Museum** (p46) and the nearby **Oregon Historical Society Museum** (p46). Then walk east to **Governor Tom McCall Waterfront Park** (p46) for a stroll along the Willamette River.

AFTERNOON

Grab lunch downtown before heading to **Forest Park** (p78) for a hike along the **Wildwood Trail** (p78), finishing at the historic **Pittock Mansion** (p82; pictured above), one of the best places to take in city views.

EVENING

Head to Southeast Portland to see what's on at the **OMSI** (Oregon Museum of Science and Industry, p106)) planetarium, or visit **Hopscotch Portland** (p110) for an evening of immersive fun.

DAY THREE

A Short Break

MORNING

A third day gives you time to get beyond Portland. Start with a bit of shopping at **Multnomah Village** (p48) in Southwest Portland, before continuing south to the Willamette Valley's wine country.

AFTERNOON

Start at **Red Hills Market** (p144) in Dundee, where you can buy gourmet treats or sit down for a filling lunch. Then head up to **Ambar Estate** (p142) in the hills west of town for a tasting experience.

EVENING

Head to the nearby city of **McMinnville** (p127; pictured above) to visit its downtown tasting rooms and grab dinner before returning to Portland.

If You Have More Time

With a bit more time in Portland and the Willamette Valley, you'll be able to really get a feel for the area. Check out offbeat attractions such as the **Portland Puppet Museum** (p111), **Mill Ends Park** (p47), the **Wishing Tree** (p36) and the **Freakybuttrue Peculiarium** (p82) and give yourself plenty of time to stroll (and shop) along NW 23rd Ave in Nob Hill and SE Hawthorne St. Make extra time in your schedule to take a scenic ride on the **Portland Aerial Tram** (p48) or head over to **McMenamins Kennedy School** (p92) to drink a beer in a former elementary school.

If you're in Portland on the first Thursday of the month, visit the **Pearl District** (p73) to check out art gallery openings; during the summer, if you're in town on the last Thursday of the month, head to the **Alberta Arts District** (p97) for a massive street fair. If your visit coincides with a weekend between March and December, don't miss the **Portland Saturday Market** (p62).

Freakybuttrue Perculiarlum display

ZUMA PRESS, INC./ALAMY

A City Day Trip

Hop in your car and head to the Oregon Coast, which is better known for its gorgeous scenery than for its weather (you're more likely to need a jacket than a swimsuit). Start with a visit to Cannon Beach, and give yourself a few hours to check out **Haystack Rock** (p121; pictured above) and browse the shops on Hemlock St. Continue south to **Tillamook** (p123) for a bit of cheese-tasting and then onwards to Lincoln City, where you can search for colorful glass floats hidden on the beach or watch glassblowing demonstrations at the **Lincoln City Glass Center** (p124) before returning to Portland.

On a Rainy Day

Portland gets a lot of rain, which means there's lots to do in the city even on the dampest of days. Powell's City of Books (p76) is a great place to while away the time if you're a reader, while fans of art and history can easily spend an afternoon between the **Portland Art Museum** (p46) and the **Oregon Historical Society Museum** (p46), which are within a few minutes' walk of each other. Other great rainy-day options include the **OMSI** (p106) and the immersive art experience **Hopscotch Portland** (p110; pictured above) both of which are loved by kids and adults alike.

Get Prepared

BOOK AHEAD

Three months before
Start looking at what events are on during your visit. Concerts and comedy shows can sell out quickly, so buy tickets early.

One month before
Make your reservations for popular restaurants such as Kann, which releases reservation slots on the first day of the prior month.

One week before
Check the weather forecast, but take it with a grain of salt – Portland weather is notoriously unpredictable.

Manners Matter

Portlanders are pretty laid-back, and interactions are typically friendly and calm. Yell-talking is frowned upon, so use your inside voice. Overly intense eye-contact or hand-crushing handshakes will make you seem obnoxious.

It's OK to be direct, but communication in Portland is more passive (and sometimes passive aggressive) than in other parts of the country. You won't hear 'please' at every interaction, but 'thank you' is expected.

Dress the Part

Most people in Portland dress for the weather, and for comfort, so there's no need to pack your shiniest shoes and your sleekest attire. Even the fanciest restaurants rarely have dress codes, so expect to see plenty of people in jeans, hoodies and tennis shoes wherever you go. Layers are always a good idea, and have a waterproof jacket at the ready.

Things to Know

Umbrellas There's a myth in Portland that umbrellas will make you stand out as a tourist. The reality is that while many residents own high-quality rain jackets that make umbrellas unnecessary, plenty of Portlanders do use them.

Bottle deposits A 10¢ bottle deposit charge is tacked on to most bottled beverages in Oregon (liquor and wine bottles are exceptions). Instead of throwing these bottles into garbage cans, place them on top. Someone will come by to collect them for redemption.

Pumping gas Until 2023, it was illegal to pump your own gas in Oregon. While self-serve is now allowed, all Portland gas stations must offer both options. Many stations have designated pumps for each; choose a 'full-service' pump if you want an attendant to do your dirty work.

TIPPING

Tipping is expected at Portland restaurants, food carts and bars, and is appreciated at cannabis dispensaries.

Restaurants
for dine-in

Bars
per drink

Coffee shops
the higher

Housekeepers
per night

DAILY BUDGET

BUDGET: Less than $150

- Dorm bed in a hostel: from $70
- Cheap meal at a food cart: $12-15
- Public transportation cap per day: $5.60

MIDRANGE: $150-400

- Standard double room with private bathroom: $125-250
- Museum or garden admission: $16 -25
- Dinner with drinks at a midrange restaurant per person: $25-50

TOP END: More than $400

- King room at a high-end hotel: $300-500
- Dinner at a fine-dining restaurant with drinks per person: $75-150
- Wine tasting in the Willamette Valley per person: from $25

TAR PICHET/SHUTTERSTOCK

TIP

The lines can get long at some of Portland's most popular food carts, but many have online ordering systems so that you can order and pay for your meal in advance.

When To Go

Portland's reputation as a rainy city isn't unfounded. Gray skies are common, save for summer when the sun shines and temperatures soar.

The weather in Portland and the Willamette Valley is generally mild, with temperatures rarely falling too far below freezing, even in the depths of winter. There's sometimes a bit of snow in January or February, but freezing rain is a bigger issue, so pay attention on the road. Spring and fall weather often bounces between cold and gray and warm and sunny, while summer can get downright hot, especially in late July and August. September wildfires are increasingly common and can bring with them poor air quality.

Major Events

May/June: Portland's biggest event, the **Portland Rose Festival** features everything from a carnival with rides to a Fleet Week, which brings American and Canadian naval ships to dock right in downtown Portland. However, it's the festival's two parades – the after-dark Starlight Parade and the Grand Floral Parade – that truly steal the show.

June/July: The city's annual **Portland Pride Waterfront Festival** celebrations sometimes take place in July, rather than during Pride Month in June, with plenty of revelry at Waterfront Park. Music lovers won't want to miss the free-for-all **Cathedral Park Jazz Festival**, the longest-running jazz and blues festival west of the Mississippi River, which brings three days of live music to Cathedral Park on the Northeast Portland riverfront.

September In true Oktoberfest style, **Mt Angel Oktoberfest** in the Willamette Valley takes place

Portland Weather

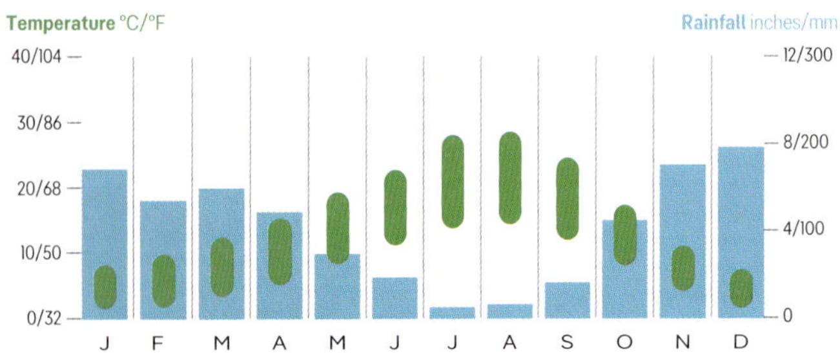

DANITA DELIMONT/ALAMY

Dancers at Mt Angel Oktoberfest

in September, bringing dirndl-clad fans of beer and pretzels to the Bavarianesque town of Mt Angel for events ranging from wiener-dog races to polka dancing.

Artsy & Whimsical

February: The dark days of winter are a little brighter thanks to the **Portland Winter Light Festival**, which brings colorful, illuminated installations to inner Portland streets over two weekends.

March/April: A 40-acre field outside of Woodburn erupts in color every spring, just in time for the **Wooden Shoe Tulip Fest**, which offers kids' activities, shopping and plenty of photo ops.

July: Near Eugene, in the southern Willamette Valley, the **Oregon Country Fair** has been keeping the spirit of the hippie generation alive with crafts and entertainment since its first edition, back in the summer of '69.

August: Watch daredevil soapbox carmakers zip down the slopes of Mt Tabor at the **Portland Adult Soapbox Derby**.

ACCOMMODATION LOWDOWN

Hotel prices tend to be higher in summer, particularly in vacation spots such as the Willamette Valley's wine country and the Oregon Coast. Weekend prices can soar in some areas, and many hotels require minimum two-night stays. Portland prices are more stable year-round.

Getting There

Portland is served by Portland International Airport (PDX) in Northeast Portland, with direct service to destinations across Oregon and beyond the US. Direct international routes are limited.

From the Airport to Downtown

MAX Light Rail

You can easily get to downtown Portland from the airport by hopping aboard the Red Line of the MAX Light Rail. The stop is just outside the south side of the terminal building and is well-signposted from both the main level of the terminal and the lower-level baggage claim area. Buy tickets from a kiosk at the end of the station closest to the terminal or tap your phone or contactless credit card on the green 'Hop' reader when you board. Trains depart roughly every 15 minutes between around 4:45am and 11:45pm.

Taxi & Rideshare

Taxis and rideshares such as Lyft and Uber meet passengers inside the airport's short-term parking garage on the main level of the airport (the same level as departures). Once you leave the secure part of the airport, follow signs to the 'Transportation Plaza' to find your ride.

Rental Car

The Rental Car Center is beside the terminal, so you won't have to wait for a shuttle to an off-site location to pick up a car.

Other Points of Entry

Union Station

Long-distance bus services operated by Greyhound and Flix Bus stop on the north side of Union Station in Portland's Old Town Chinatown neighborhood, offering service to Seattle and beyond. The Oregon Department of Transportation's POINT inter-city bus connects Union Station cities and towns across the state, including Woodburn, Salem, Albany and Eugene for the Willamette Valley, plus Bend, Ashland, Medford and destinations up and down the Oregon Coast.

Amtrak

Trains stop at Union Station, with direct connections to the Green, Yellow and Orange Lines of the MAX Light Rail and the A Loop of the Portland Streetcar.

Getting Around

Portland's public transportation system is excellent, with a mix of bus, light-rail trains and streetcar service connecting most parts of the compact city. Renting a car is a great option if you plan to explore areas outside the city center, and parking is usually abundant.

Car Rentals

Although Portland has a fantastic public transportation system, renting a car can be your best option for getting around town. Street parking is free in much of the city, though you'll need to pay to park in Downtown, the Pearl District, Old Town, Chinatown and parts of Southeast and Nob Hill. Getting further afield, particularly in the Willamette Valley, can be challenging without your own car.

Rideshare & Taxis

If you don't drive or are staying in downtown Portland, you may find rideshares, such as Lyft and Uber, or taxis a more convenient option for getting around town. **Radio Cab** *(radiocab.net; 503-227-1212)* and **Broadway Cab** *(broadwaycab.com; 503-333-3333)* are Portland's most established taxi companies.

TriMet

The public transportation system in Portland and surrounding areas is managed by TriMet. The network consists of a large number of bus lines along with five MAX Light Rail lines, each with its own color. The tram system is called the Portland Streetcar, which has tickets integrated with TriMet, so you won't have to pay a separate fare if you're transferring between the two systems.

FROM LEFT: BANDERSNATCH/SHUTTERSTOCK, QUIGGYT4/SHUTTERSTOCK

ESSENTIAL APP

Download the **Parking Kitty** *(parkingkitty.com)* app to quickly and easily pay for parking at Portland meters.

Bicycles & E-Scooters

Portland is famously bicycle friendly, with an extensive network of dedicated lanes, the newest of which are painted green. Special green-colored crossings at standard crosswalks are meant specifically for cyclists, and some parts of town have green 'bike boxes' painted on the roads in front of traffic lights; cars are expected to stop before these boxes, as only cyclists are allowed to use them. Cyclists are expected to obey all traffic laws and must always yield to pedestrians. Similar rules and regulations apply to e-scooters.

Local bike-rental operators include **Cycle Portland** *(portlandbicycletours.com)* and **Everybody's Bike Rentals** *(pdxbikerentals.com)*. You can also rent bicycles through the **Biketown** *(biketownpdx.com)* bike-share program, which has stations around town, and e-scooters through **Lime** *(li.me)*.

Public Transportation Essentials

Payment Options

You can use credit or debit cards with contactless payment capabilities or your phone's mobile wallet (using Google Pay, Samsung Pay or Apple Pay) to pay for an adult fare by simply tapping them on a 'Hop reader' inside the bus (or, if you're taking the MAX Light Rail, on the station platform). To pay for Youth or Honored Citizen fares, you'll need to either download TriMet's **Hop app** *(myhopcard.com)* or obtain a physical Hop Card (available at most local grocery stores and at special card dispensers found at MAX stations around the city). Note that cards cost $3 and you can reload them wherever they are sold. There's a $5 minimum to reload, except at the TriMet Office at Downtown's Pioneer Courthouse Square and at Hop Card vending machines.

You can also use cash to pay for bus fare; just tell your driver whether you want a 2½-hour ticket or an all-day pass. Coins and bills are accepted, but drivers can't give you change, so make sure you have the exact fare.

Daily & Monthly Caps

For adults aged 18 to 64, it costs $2.80 to ride any combination of MAX, bus and streetcar lines for up to 2½ hours, with daily fares capped at $5.60 (after which you ride free). The monthly cap for adult ticket-holders is $100 per calendar month.

TriMet also offers a Youth Fare for kids aged seven to 17 (children under six ride free) as well as a special Honored Citizen fare category that applies to people 65 and older, those on Medicare, people with disabilities or income-based qualifications, veterans and active-duty military. Travelers in both categories pay $1.40 for 2½ hours and are capped at $2.80 per day or $28 per month.

FARE EVASION

Getting caught without a valid ticket can result in a $75 fine (for first-time offenders).

GETTING TO THE WILLAMETTE VALLEY FROM PORTLAND

You can get from Portland to select destinations in the Willamette Valley without a car. All southbound Amtrak trains stop in Salem and Albany, as does the Cascades Route of the POINT bus. You can also take Yamhill County Transit bus 44 from TriMet's Tigard Transit Center near SW Portland all the way to McMinnville; the route stops in Newberg and Dundee along the way.

ACCESSIBLE FOR ALL

Portland's public buses, street cars and light-rail trains are wheelchair accessible, with boarding ramps or power lifts. Features for blind and low-vision riders include textured tiles for white cane users, braille and raised-letter signage, and audio announcements at select stations. For more info, visit *trimet.org/access*.

A Few Surprises

Portland is a place where the unconventional is celebrated, which means you're sure to find plenty of fun surprises.

Sidewalk Horse Rings

Once upon a time, most Portlanders got around town on horseback or in horse-drawn carriages. Instead of metered parking spots, city sidewalks had metal tethering loops known as horse rings embedded in sidewalks, which made it easy for people to tie up their steeds while they went about their business. Horses were, of course, later replaced by motor vehicles, and the city began tearing out the old rings every time they replaced sidewalks. Portlanders, who aren't always too thrilled about change, protested, which led to a rule that the rings must be replaced whenever sidewalks are repaired or replaced. These days, the rings are used to tether model horses.

In 2005, a resident named Scott Wayne Indiana decided to make the most of these rings, launching the **Portland Horse Project** *(#portlandhorseproject)*, which encourages Portlanders to tether toy horses to every ring they see. If you have a spare plastic horse in need of a good home, consider bringing it with you on your Portland trip and tying it onto a horse ring yourself. You'll find the rings all over the inner east side of the city.

Little Free Everything

You may have seen Little Free Libraries, roadside mini-libraries where visitors can pick up a new book or leave an old one behind. While there are plenty of these in Portland, residents have taken things a step further, which means there are plenty of other 'Little Free' things to be found around town. Head to **SE 78th and Morrison** to find both a mug exchange and Dinorama, a toy dinosaur

OFFBEAT PORTLAND

Put on a costume for free entry to **Freakybuttrue Peculiarium**, where you can see all sorts of oddities.

Look for the rumored resident leprechauns at **Mill Ends Park**, the second-tiniest park on Earth.

Write a wish on a tag and tie it to the **Wishing Tree**, a magical tree that helps bring dreams to fruition.

See a huge selection of puppets from around the world at the **Portland Puppet Museum**.

Horse ring

exchange. Both are the creations of Rachael Harm Mahlandt, who's also created the **Worldwide Sidewalk Joy Map** *(worldwidsidewalkjoy.com)*, where you can find sidewalk exchanges and displays across Portland and around the world. Other little free treats locally include seed libraries for gardeners, toy libraries for families and plenty of fetching-stick libraries (often with treats and drinking water) for the four-legged set.

Painted Intersections

If you find yourself strolling through a Southeast Portland neighborhood, don't be surprised if you come across a gargantuan, multihued mandala in the middle of a four-way intersection. These colorful creations, designed to add a little joy and brightness to neighborhood streets, are usually the work of the **City Repair Project** *(cityrepair.org)*, a nonprofit organization that's on a mission to inspire residents to use creativity to make their communities more livable and fun. One of the oldest - and best known - is the **Sunnyside Piazza** on the corner of SE 33rd and Yamhill. While the first thing you're likely to notice here is a giant, sunflower-like design that stretches across the intersection and up onto the sidewalk, there's also a community information kiosk where neighbors can post notices and cob benches where you can take a load off.

Explore Portland

Downtown & Southwest Portland....... 41
Washington Park 54
Old Town Chinatown 59
Northwest Portland & Pearl District...73
Northeast & North Portland 89
Southeast Portland 103
McMinnville 127
Newberg & Dundee 139
Salem..149

Worth a Trip

The Columbia River Gorge 116
The Oregon Coast 120
Oregon City 146
Mt Angel 158

Portland's Walking Tours

Downtown Portland 44
Old Town Chinatown 66
Pearl District 80
Northeast Portland 94
Southeast Portland 108
McMinnville 132

Pioneer Courthouse Square (p46)
IAN DAGNALL/ALAMY

See p50 for eating, drinking and shopping listings

Explore Downtown & Southwest Portland

Researched by Margot Bigg

On the western side of the Willamette River sits Portland's compact downtown, an area characterized as much by its tree-lined parks and brick plazas as it is by its towering office buildings. It's here where you'll find the bulk of Portland's cultural attractions, as well as its fanciest hotels. Although downtown is part of Southwest Portland, most residents use the term 'Southwest' to refer to the predominantly residential areas beyond the city center. Head out to this hilly, semi-forested part of town to visit Multnomah Village, a compact shopping 'village' packed with independent shops, pubs and restaurants.

Getting Around

Bus

Downtown Portland is the main transit hub for the entire city, and most city bus lines stop here. Northbound buses typically stop on 6th Ave, while southbound routes stop on 5th Ave.

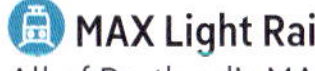

MAX Light Rail

All of Portland's MAX lines stop downtown. The Red Line connects downtown with the airport, while the Red and Blue Lines offer direct service to Washington Park.

Streetcar

The A and B Loops and North-South Lines of the Portland Streetcar serve downtown Portland.

THE BEST

TRANQUIL GARDEN
Portland Japanese Garden (p54)

ART MUSEUM
Portland Art Museum (p46)

PEOPLE-WATCHING PERCH
Pioneer Courthouse Sq (p46)

PLACE FOR A STROLL
Governor Tom McCall Waterfront Park (p46)

LEPRECHAUN'S LAIR
Mill Ends Park (p47)

South Park Block (p44)

MIKER/SHUTTERSTOCK

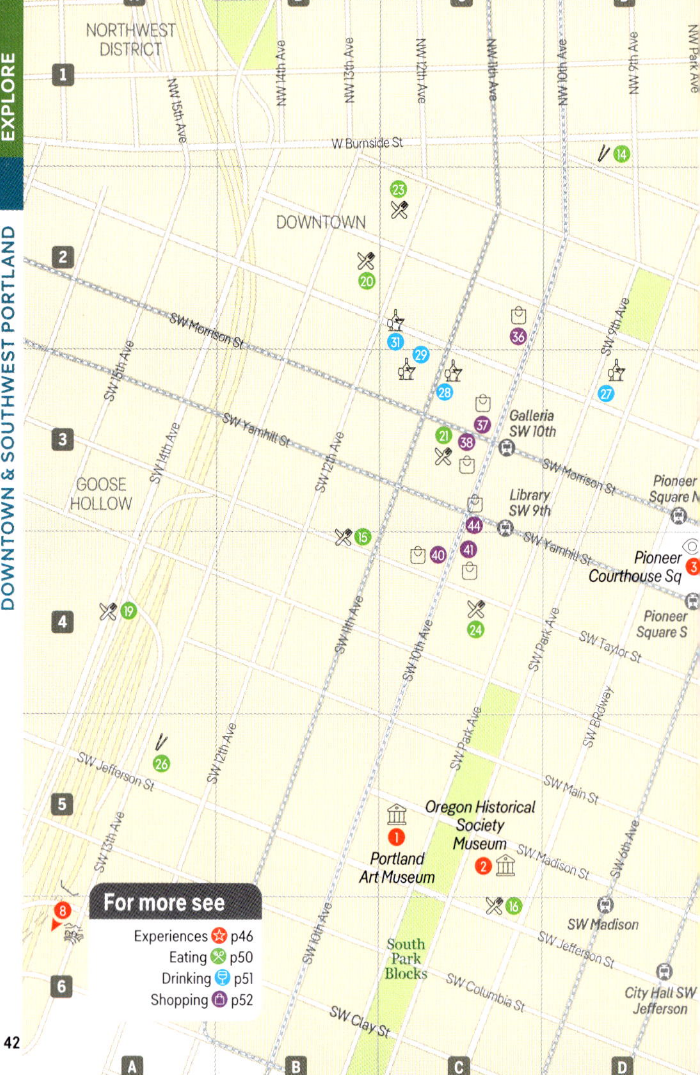
NORTHWEST DISTRICT
DOWNTOWN
GOOSE HOLLOW
W Burnside St
SW Morrison St
SW Yamhill St
SW Taylor St
SW Main St
SW Madison St
SW Jefferson St
SW Columbia St
SW Clay St
NW 15th Ave
NW 14th Ave
NW 13th Ave
NW 12th Ave
NW 11th Ave
NW 10th Ave
NW 9th Ave
NW Park Ave
SW 15th Ave
SW 14th Ave
SW 13th Ave
SW 12th Ave
SW 11th Ave
SW 10th Ave
SW 9th Ave
SW Park Ave
SW BRdway
SW 6th Ave
Galleria SW 10th
Library SW 9th
Pioneer Square N
Pioneer Courthouse Sq
Pioneer Square S
SW Madison
City Hall SW Jefferson
Oregon Historical Society Museum
Portland Art Museum
South Park Blocks
For more see
Experiences p46
Eating p50
Drinking p51
Shopping p52

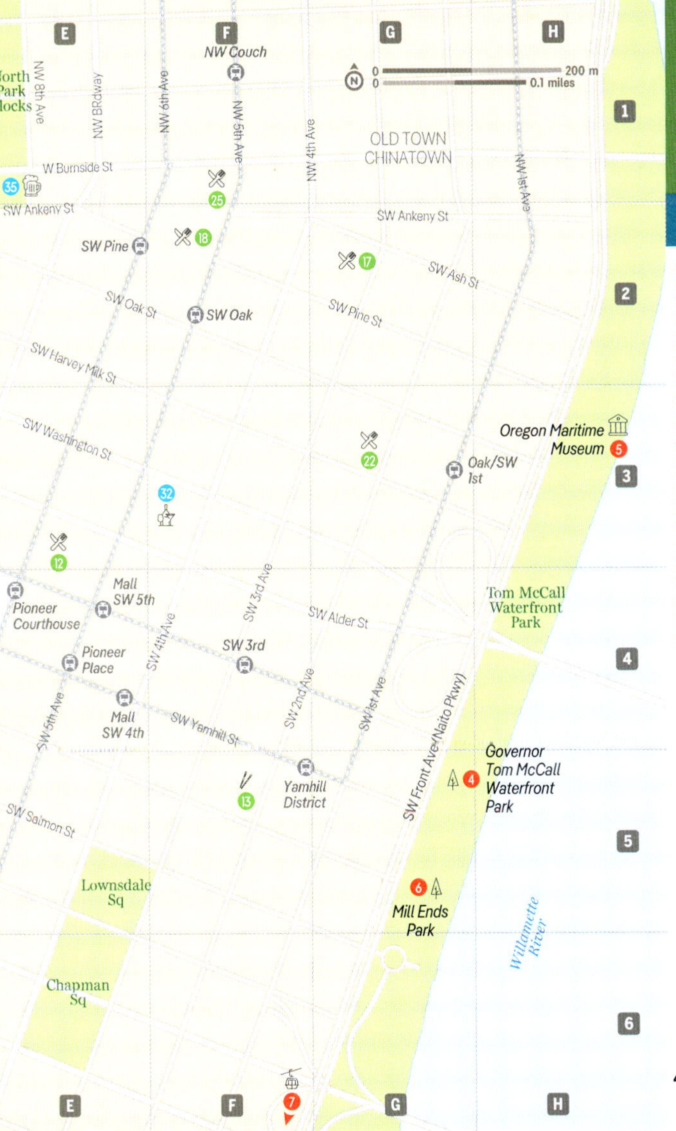

EXPLORE

DOWNTOWN & SOUTHWEST PORTLAND

WALKING TOUR

Walk Downtown Portland

Although downtown Portland feels fairly quiet, owing largely to a post-pandemic shift to remote working, it's still Portland's urban hub. This walk takes you past towering office buildings and through grassy parks and red-brick plazas, offering plenty of opportunities along the way to stop and take in the scenery.

START	END	LENGTH
Portland Visitor Center	Pioneer Courthouse Sq	1.8 miles; 1 hour

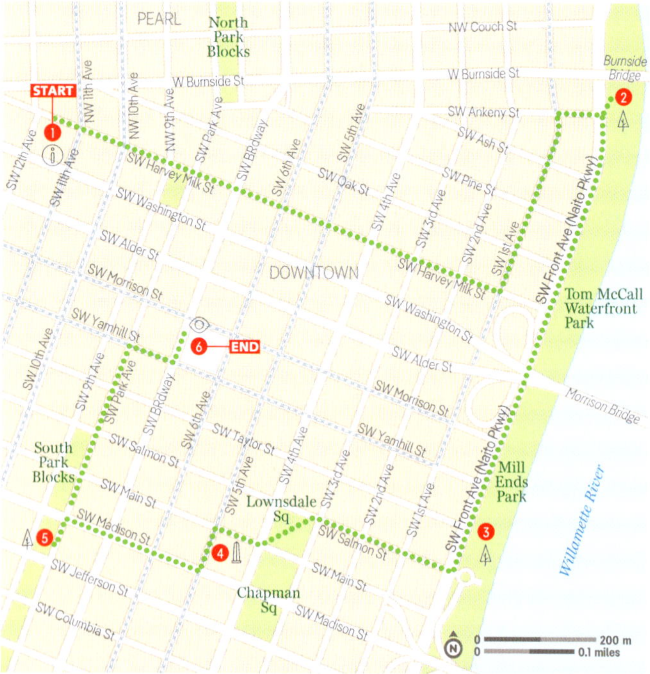

1 Get Acquainted

Start at the **Portland Visitor Center**, where you can pick up free souvenir stickers and brochures, fill up your water bottle, charge your phone or ask questions from visitor-center staff. From here, walk east along SW Harvey Milk St until you reach Naito Pkwy, which runs parallel to the Willamette River.

2 Down by the River

Flanking the banks of the Willamette River, grassy **Governor Tom McCall Waterfront Park** – or 'Waterfront' as residents call it – is your next stop. If you visit on a weekend, head north to check out craft vendors at Portland Saturday Market; otherwise, head south for a walk along the riverfront park, taking in views of city bridges and passing boats along the way.

3 Leprechaun Land

Continue to the first crosswalk at SW Taylor St and start walking away from the river and back into the high-rise-dotted blocks of central downtown. In the middle of the intersection is **Mill Ends Park**, the world's second-smallest park, complete with its own official Portland Parks & Recreation sign. According to a decades-old urban legend, leprechauns live here.

4 The Real Portlandia

Walk for about six blocks until you reach the **Portland Building**, a hodgepodge of windows, sharp angles and bow-like adornments; it's considered a masterpiece of post-modern architecture. On a ledge overlooking the entryway kneels *Portlandia*, a gargantuan statue depicting a goddess wielding a trident that also happens to be the second-largest copper repoussé statue in the US (the Statue of Liberty is the largest).

5 Park Life

Continue west for a few more blocks and you'll soon find yourself in the **South Park Blocks**, a 12-block stretch of urban park that's also home to many of the city's top cultural institutions. Highlights include the sprawling Portland Art Museum and the Oregon Historical Society Museum. Farmers markets take place in the park every Wednesday and Saturday.

6 Portland's True Center

Nicknamed 'Portland's Living Room,' **Pioneer Courthouse Square** does very much feel like the Rose City's gathering place. Wrap your tour up by getting a selfie with *Allow Me* (aka *Umbrella Man*), a life-size bronze statue of a man with an umbrella in the southwest quadrant of the square.

EXPERIENCES

Expose Yourself to Art at the Portland Art Museum MUSEUM

MAP: 1 P42 **C5**

Established in 1892, the **Portland Art Museum** *(portlandartmuseum.org; adult/child $25/free)* is the oldest art museum in the Pacific Northwest and the largest in Oregon, with over 112,000 sq ft of gallery space. Give yourself at least an hour to explore its mix of temporary and permanent exhibits, which showcase art and artifacts from across the region and beyond, with pieces by world-renowned artists such as Claude Monet and Diego Rivera in the permanent collection. The museum also houses the **Confederated Tribes of Grand Ronde Center for Native American Art**, which displays a massive collection of North American indigenous art. Free admission on the first Thursday of the month.

Explore the Past at the Oregon Historical Society MUSEUM

MAP: 2 P42 **C5**

Across from the Portland Art Museum, the **Oregon Historical Society Museum** *(ohs.org/museum; adult/child $14/free)* provides a great introduction to the history of the region through **Experience Oregon**, an interactive permanent exhibit that tells the state's story. Highlights of this 7000-sq-ft exhibit include a replica of an Oregon Trail–era covered wagon and interpretive displays about the many communities that shaped the state into what it is today. You can also see the penny that determined Portland's name through a simple coin flip (Boston was the losing candidate).

Watch Passersby at Pioneer Square PARK

MAP: 3 P42 **D4**

Nicknamed 'Portland's living room,' **Pioneer Courthouse Square** *(thesquarepdx.org; free)* is a great place to people-watch, especially if you come during the summer, when sunny weather brings in big crowds. This central plaza is made entirely of red bricks – tens of thousands of them – many of which bear the engraved names of those who have sponsored them (you can get your own brick for a $150 donation). 'The Square,' as it's locally nicknamed, hosts a regular schedule of concerts and cultural festivals all summer. However, it's the annual **Christmas tree-lighting ceremony**, which features a massive tree adorned by veteran Portland production company Hollywood Lights, that draws in the big crowds.

Wander Alongside the River at Waterfront Park PARK

Stretching alongside the western banks of the Willamette River for over a mile, **Governor Tom McCall Waterfront Park** (MAP: 4 P43 **G5**) is a great place to go for a stroll or a jog while taking in views of some of Portland's many bridges. A good place to start is directly under the Burnside Bridge, which divides the northern and southern parts of the city, before heading south, continuing all the way to Salmon Street Springs, a massive fountain that doubles as a splash pad for Portland kids on sweltering summer days. Along the way, you'll pass the Battleship Oregon Memorial, which honors the USS Oregon (BB-3), one of the nation's first modern battleships, and the **Oregon Maritime Museum** (MAP: 5 P43 **H3**; *oregonmaritimemuseum.org; adult/child $10/5),* a historic sternwheeler that doubles as a museum and is open on Thursday and Saturday afternoons.

If you're visiting Portland in the summer, there may be an event taking place at Waterfront Park. Popular annual events include the May - June **Portland Rose Festival City Fair** *(rosefestival.org),* the June or July **Portland Pride Waterfront Festival** *(portlandpride.org)* and the July **Waterfront Blues Festival** *(waterfrontbluesfest.com).*

Look for Leprechauns at Mill Ends Park

PARK

MAP: 6 P43 **G5**

Not all of Portland's parks are sprawling. In fact, the city is home to the world's second-smallest park, Mill Ends Park, which sits smack in the middle of a median strip at the corner of SW Naito Pkwy and Taylor St, mere steps from Waterfront Park. At 452 sq inches, the miniature park was the Guinness World Records-approved smallest park in the world until 2025, when it was usurped by an even smaller park in Japan. This tiny park – which, like other parks in Portland, is managed by Portland Parks & Recreation – features a scaled-down park sign and typically has a few miniatures within its bounds. According to local lore, leprechauns live in this tiny patch of park. However, these little beings are as shy as they are wee, and thus may be hiding during your visit.

DOWNTOWN FARMERS MARKETS

Downtown Portland is home to two of the city's top farmers markets. The best-known farmers market takes place at the Portland State University campus, along the southern part of a 12-block park called the South Park Blocks. Held every Saturday, rain or shine, this massive market brings out loads of regional farmers who sell everything from fresh fruit and flowers to massive loaves of freshly baked bread. A smaller market is held on the northern end of the South Park Blocks, in front of the Portland Art Museum, on Wednesdays from May to October.

Fly High on the Portland Aerial Tram

CABLE CAR

MAP: 7 P43 **F6**

Connecting Portland's South Waterfront neighborhood to Oregon Health & Science University (OHSU), a teaching hospital on top of Marquam Hill, the Portland Aerial Tram *(gobytram.com; $8.50/ round trip)* is both a practical means of public transportation and a great way to take views of the skyline. The trip in this standing-room-only aerial tram, which doesn't operate on Sundays or holidays, lasts around four minutes in each direction. It's easiest to start at the base of the hill, where there's parking and a Portland Streetcar stop. Unless you have a doctor's appointment, you'll probably just want to go to the top of the hill, turn around and come back down again, but be prepared for waits if you travel during rush hour. Notice that the tram cars are shaped like giant silver pills, which is fitting given that more people know Marquam Hill by its moniker – Pill Hill. The jury is out on whether this choice was by design or fluke.

Stroll Through Multnomah Village

SHOPPING DISTRICT

A 5-mile drive south of downtown will take you to Portland's very own village within a city, Multnomah Village (MAP: 8 P42 **A6** and P49). This compact shopping district is as adorable as the name suggests, featuring a few blocks of independent shops, many of which have been operating for generations, plus some fabulous restaurants. One of the oldest businesses in the village, Annie Bloom's Books (p66), is also one of the city's top literary haunts, offering regular readings by local and nationally acclaimed authors. Other highlights include **Thinker Toys** (MAP: 9 P49 **C3**; *thinkertoystore.com)*, which has been selling charming educational toys in the village since the 1990s, and **Village Coffee** (MAP: 10 P49 **C3**), a compact cafe serving tasty organic brews. If you're more of a beer drinker, head over to **John's Marketplace** (MAP: 11 P49 **B4**; *johnsmarketplace.com)*, a specialty supermarket and beer shop with a spacious outdoor patio where visitors can imbibe freely.

THE PORTLAND SPIRIT

A great way to see Portland, and its famous bridges, is from right on the water aboard the **Portland Spirit** *(portlandspirit.com; from $69)*, a double-decker sailing yacht with a restaurant and an open-air viewing deck. This urban cruise line specializes in brunch, lunch and dinner cruises that run year-round, no matter the season. Most cruises last two to 2½ hours and travel from downtown Portland clear down to the neighboring city of Lake Oswego and back again, passing below nine one-of-a-kind city bridges along the way.

For more see

Drinking p51
Shopping p52

A B C D E F
1 2 3 4

SW 32nd Ave
SW 33rd Ave
SW 34th Ave
SW 35th Ave
SW Capitol Hwy

9 Thinker Toys
10 Village Coffee
11 John's Marketplace
30
33
34
39
42
43
45

0 100 m
0 0.05 miles

LISTINGS

Best Places for...

$ Budget $$ Midrange $$$ Top End

See p42 for map of locations, unless specified.

Eating

Asian

Departure $$$
12 E3
On the top floor of the Nines Hotel, this sleek spot pairs pan-Asian cuisine and fancy cocktails with great views of the city, especially from its outdoor decks. *departureportland.com; 4-11pm*

Luc Lac Vietnamese Kitchen $$
13 F5
Pho, bánh mì and Vietnamese-inspired bowls draw big crowds (and, sometimes, long lines) to this hip spot in the heart of the city. *luclackitchen.com; 11am-2:30pm & 4-11pm*

Thai Peacock $$
14 D1
Thai classics get a creative spin at this beloved restaurant where you can get pad Thai served with crispy trout or fried rice paired with pineapple pork. *thaipeacockpdx.com; 11:30am-9pm Sun-Thu, to 10pm Fri & Sat*

American

Daily Feast $
15 B4
This all-American diner with a modern twist serves a simple menu of American breakfast classics in the morning and burgers and salads at lunch. *thedailyfeastpdx.com; 7am-2pm Mon-Fri, to 3pm Sat & Sun*

Higgins $$$
16 C6
Among the oldest fine-dining restaurants in downtown Portland, this Pacific Northwest spot can surely credit its staying power to consistent quality and innovative menus that showcase the bounty of local farms. *higginsportland.com; hours vary Tue-Sun*

Mother's Bistro $$
17 G2
Homestyle gets an upscale touch at this bright restaurant. Come in the morning for a hearty scramble or plate of pancakes, or visit later in the day for a huge salad or filling burger. *mothersbistro.com; lunch 9am-2pm, dinner hours vary*

Portland City Grill $$$
18 F2
Take in city views at this upscale spot on the 30th floor of the US Bank Tower (aka the 'Big Pink'), the second-highest building in the city. *portlandcitygrill.com; hours vary*

Indian

Dil Se $$
19 A4
Choose from a huge menu of North and South Indian classics, plus a few Indo-Chinese favorites, at this downtown spot. *dilsepdx.com; 11am-2:30pm Tue-Sun, 4-9pm Fri & Sat*

Italian

Dolly Olive $$$

20 B2
Dine on Southern Italian dishes of fresh veggies, focaccia, seafood and more at this modern spot, part of Portland's beloved

Sesame Collective group of restaurants. *sesamecollective.com/dollyolive; hours vary*

Mucca Osteria $$$

 C3

Celebrate a special night at this intimate fine-dining restaurant with a dinner of handmade pasta paired with delicious wine. *muccaosteria.com; 5-10pm*

Middle Eastern

Al-Amir Restaurant $$

 G3

Exposed brick paired with Arabesque decor adds extra oomph to the ambience at this Lebanese spot, but it's the tasty kebabs, baba ghanoush and more that keeps diners coming back. *alamirportland.com; 5-9pm Wed-Sat*

Seafood

Jake's Famous Crawfish $$$

 C2

One of the oldest restaurants in the city, Jake's has been serving seafood to hungry Portlanders since 1892. Don't miss the crawfish étouffée. *jakesfamous.com; 11:30am-9pm Sun-Thu, to 10pm Fri & Sat*

Southpark Seafood $$$

 C4

This sleek spot at the base of the South Park Blocks is beloved for its oyster bar and its great cocktails. *southparkseafood.com; 11:30am-8:30pm Mon-Fri, to 3pm Sat & Sun*

Vegan & Vegetarian

Rabbits Cafe $

 F1

Most vegetarians and vegans have had their meals jokingly referred to as 'rabbit food' at some point. Turns out that rabbits are onto something, as you'll quickly learn when you dig into a nutritious and filling bowl or scramble at this spot in the lobby of the 'Big Pink' (US Bank Tower) office building. *rabbitspdx.com; 8am-2pm Mon-Fri*

Walk the Wok $$

 A5

Enjoy plant-based takes on Chinese favorites at this spot, which was formerly run under the international vegan Loving Hut umbrella. The Golden Yum Melt – seafood-inspired cream-cheese-stuffed wontons – are enough to merit a visit. *walkthewokor.com; hours vary Tue-Sun*

Drinking

Cocktails

Abigail Hall

 D3

Sit down for a strong cocktail or fragrant mocktail or treat yourself to afternoon tea at this feminine, vintage-inspired cocktail spot. *abigailhallpdx.com; 5-11pm Mon-Sat, 6-11pm Sun*

Fortune

 C3

Tasty cocktails, fortune tellers and regular DJ events are among the big draws of this dimly lit hotel bar in downtown Portland. *fortune.bar; 4pm-midnight Sun-Thu, to 2am Fri & Sat*

Green Room

 C3

If you don't have a reservation at the Multnomah Whiskey Library, you can still sample some of the highlights of its cocktail program at this sister bar on the ground floor of the same building. The green stained-glass ceiling adds to the ambience. *mwlpdx.com/the-green-room; 4-11:30pm Tue-Sat, to 12:30am Fri & Sat*

Gibson

30 E2 on P49 map

Add a bit of mid-century flair to your happy hour at this cocktail bar in Multnomah Village. *instagram .com/thegibsonpdx; 4-10pm Sun-Thu, to midnight Fri & Sat*

Multnomah Whiskey Library

31 C2

You'll need to buy a 'hall pass' to visit this members' club, where bottles from a 1500-spirit collection are displayed in floor-to-ceiling bookshelves, complete with library ladders. *mwlpdx. com; 4-10pm Tue-Sat*

Dive

Kelly's Olympian

32 F3

One of the oldest bars in Portland, this gritty downtown spot is nothing like your typical Portland craft-cocktail spot. Live music and DJ sets rile up the crowds on select evenings. *kellysolympian. com; 5pm-2am Tue & Wed, 1pm-2am Thu-Sun*

Ship Tavern

33 B3 on P49 map

Among the cute shops and restaurants in Multnomah Village, this longstanding neighborhood bar has pool tables and two dozen beers on tap. *mvship.com; 11am-midnight Sun-Thu, to 2am Fri & Sat*

Pub

Proper Pint Oakroom

34 F2 on P49 map

Beer-lovers will find lots to choose from at this Multnomah Village spot with a massive tap list. Dogs are welcome, too. *properpintoakroom.com; hours vary*

Rachel & Rose

35 E1

Stop in for a pint or your tipple of choice at this big red bar, which is housed in a converted double-decker bus that was shipped all the way from London. *rachelspub. com; 2-8pm Tue-Sat, to 9pm Fri & Sat*

Shopping

Apparel

Frances May

36 C2

Find apparel for men and women, much of it made by local designers, at this downtown boutique. *francesmay.com; 11am-6pm Mon-Sat, to 5pm Sun*

Kiriko Made

37 C3

High-quality, minimalist apparel made from Japanese textiles make Kiriko Made a great stop for fashion-lovers, while imported housewares and accessories make it a must for anyone looking for unique gift items. *kirikomade.com; 11am-6pm Sun-Thu, to 7pm Fri-Sun*

SaySay Boutique

38 C3

Adorable dresses, many with pockets, are enough to merit a visit to this friendly downtown boutique. *saysayboutique. bigcartel.com; 11am-6pm Mon-Sat, to 4pm Sun*

Books

Annie Bloom's

39 B3 on P49 map

In the heart of Multnomah Village, this longstanding independent bookstore offers a wide selection of titles from local and international authors and a fantastic selection of magazines, journals and greeting cards. *annie blooms.com; 9am-9pm Mon-Fri, to 7pm Sat, to 6pm Sun*

Friends Library Store

40 C4

While Portland is famous for Powell's, bibliophiles in the know head to this charity bookstore that benefits the county library to find used books (including retired library tomes). *friends-library.org/store; noon-5pm Fri & Sat*

Grand Gesture

41 C4

Calling all Fabio fans to this romance bookstore, the first of its kind in Portland, which may have you clutching your pearls. *instagram.com/grandgesturebooks; 11am-5pm Tue-Sun*

Gifts & Decor

Indigo Traders

42 B3 on P49 map

Shop for homewares from Turkey and across the Mediterranean at this neighborhood store in Multnomah Village. Enjoy free Turkish coffee while you browse. *indigotraders.com; 11am-6pm Mon-Sat, to 4pm Sun*

JP General

43 A3 on P49 map

Add a bit of understated elegance to your home or garden at this neighborhood spot, which also offers an excellent range of jewelry. *jpgeneralshop.com; 10am-5pm Mon-Thu, to 6pm Fri & Sat, 11am-4pm Sun*

Crafty Wonderland

44 C3

Support local makers by shopping at the downtown branch of this shop specializing in homemade gifts and apparel made in and around Portland. *craftywonderland.com; 11am-5pm*

Peggy Sundays

45 A4 on P49 map

Pick up homewares, toiletries and gifts for all ages at this little shop in SW Portland's pint-sized Multnomah Village. *peggysundays.com; 11am-6pm Mon-Fri, to 5:30pm Sat, to 4pm Sun*

★ TOP EXPERIENCE

Washington Park

On a hill overlooking downtown Portland, Washington Park is a 410-acre park that's home to a mix of beautiful gardens, trail-lined woodlands and some of Portland's best outdoor attractions. It's also the starting point of the Wildwood Trail, a 30-mile trail that connects it to neighboring Forest Park (p78).

MAP **P56**

GETTING THERE
Paid parking is available in lots throughout the park. To get to the park using public transport, take the Red or Blue Line of the MAX Light Rail or bus route 15 or 20.

Scan for information.

International Rose Test Garden

See why Portland is nicknamed the 'City of Roses' at the **International Rose Test Garden** *(free)*, the oldest continuously operated garden of its kind in the US. The garden is home to over 10,000 rose bushes and more than 610 varieties of rose, with new varieties added every year. There's also a small garden store where you can pick up rose-themed souvenirs and gifts. While the best time to visit is between May and October, when the garden is at its most colorful and fragrant, it's worth stopping by no matter what time of year you're in Portland to take in views of downtown Portland against the backdrop of perpetually snowcapped Mt Hood.

Portland Japanese Garden

Spread across 12 acres on a hilltop above the rose garden, the **Portland Japanese Garden** *(japanesegarden.org; adult/child $22.50/16.50)* is considered one of the most authentic gardens of its type outside Japan. A long path leads up to the garden's **Cultural Village** (shuttles are also available for visitors unable to make the steep trek). Here you'll find a courtyard with a gift shop, a cafe, a library and exhibit spaces showcasing Japanese art. A

INGE JOHNSSON/ALAMY

gate at the far end of the courtyard leads to the gardens themselves, which feature narrow paths that weave past koi ponds crossed with stone bridges and plenty of impeccably manicured foliage. Highlights include the **Tea Garden** with a traditional tea house and the **Sand and Stone Garden**, which comprises large rocks and perfectly raked gravel (think a life-size version of desktop 'Zen gardens'). Volunteer-led public tours take place on most days and are included in the cost of admission, but space is limited, so it's best to reserve your spot online ahead of your visit.

Into the Woods

Although much of Washington Park consists of pretty gardens and big green expanses, there are also plenty of woodsy features (this is Portland, after all). See trees from across the planet at the

QUICK BREAK
The Japanese Garden's **Umami Café** serves traditional Japanese teas such as matcha, sencha and mugicha along with miso soup and mochi ice cream flights.

0 500 m
0 0.25 miles
W Burnside St
Oregon Holocaust Memorial
SW Fairview Blvd
ARLINGTON HEIGHTS
Umami Café
International Rose Test Garden
Wildwood Trail
Portland Japanese Garden
Wildwood Trail
Hoyt Arboretum
Hoyt Arboretum Visitor Center
SW Sherwood Blvd
SYLVAN-HIGHLANDS
SW Kingston Dr
SW Fairview Blvd
Wildwood Trail
Washington Park
Wildwood Trail
World Forestry Center Discovery Museum
Washington Park
SOUTHWEST HILLS
SW Montgomery Dr
Oregon Zoo
SW Knights Blvd
SW Upper Dr

Hoyt Arboretum *(hoytarboretum.org; free)*, a 'living museum' featuring more than 2300 tree species from six continents. The best way to explore this 189-acre expanse is by heading to the **Visitor Center**, where you can get information about must-see trees (or get a trail map). Free guided tours take place on Sundays (April to October) at 11am; tours on the first Sunday of the month are designed with accessibility in mind and stick to paved trails.

From the Visitor Center, it's a 15-minute walk (or two-minute shuttle ride) to the **World Forestry Center Discovery Museum** *(worldforestry.org; adult/child $8/5)*, which features two floors of interactive exhibits that cover forestry-related topics ranging from forest fires to wildlife. Don't miss the vintage steam locomotive, 'Peggy the Train,' whose original purpose when she was built in 1909 was to haul logs through Pacific Northwest forests.

Elsewhere in the Park

Other Washington Park highlights include tennis courts and a playground (both near the International Rose Test Garden), an archery range, and acres of open fields, some with picnic benches, as well as the **Oregon Zoo** *(oregonzoo.org)*, known for its Asian elephants and a breeding program that's not without controversy. On the northeastern side of the park is the **Oregon Holocaust Memorial**, which features bronze cast objects such as an old violin, a book and a child's teddy bear strewn across stone paths, symbolizing the left-behind items of Jewish people who were kidnapped and sent to concentration camps. A large memorial wall honors the relatives of Oregonians and Southwest Washingtonians who were killed during the Holocaust.

THE WASHINGTON PARK FREE SHUTTLE LOOP

The easiest way to get around Washington Park is aboard the park's free, wheelchair-accessible shuttle, which runs every 15 to 30 minutes throughout the year (9:30am–7pm April to September; 10am–4pm October to March). The shuttle runs from the MAX Light Rail station and makes additional stops at key points of interest in the park, including the Hoyt Arboretum and the International Rose Test Garden.

See p70 for eating, drinking and shopping listings

Researched by Margot Bigg

Explore Old Town Chinatown

Portland's oldest neighborhood, Old Town Chinatown is also the city's grittiest. While the first thing you're likely to notice is the stone and brick facades of historic buildings, many nearly as old as Portland itself, you'll likely also notice a fair amount of litter, as well as makeshift encampments that provide shelter to the neighborhood's noticeable population of unhoused people. Although these factors can deter people from visiting Old Town Chinatown, there are also plenty of things to draw visitors in, from museums that tell the story of the Asian American communities that helped build this area to one of Portland's most spectacular gardens.

Getting Around

Walking

Old Town Chinatown is compact, and walking from point to point is the fastest and most effective way to get around.

MAX Light Rail

Take the Red or Blue Line of the MAX Light Rail to the Old Town Chinatown or Skidmore Fountain stop for easy access to the neighborhood. The Green, Yellow and Orange Lines make multiple stops along 5th and 6th Aves.

Bus

Numerous city buses stop in the Old Town Chinatown area, including lines 4, 8, 16, 35, 40, 44 and 77.

THE BEST

CRAFTY MARKET Portland Saturday Market (p62)

DRAG QUEEN REVIEW Darcelle XV Showplace (p69)

PINBALL PARADISE Ground Kontrol Classic Arcade and Bar (p68)

TRANQUIL GARDEN Lan Su Chinese Garden (p64)

HISTORY MUSEUM Portland Chinatown Museum (p68)

Chinatown Gateway (p67)

ARTYOORAN/SHUTTERSTOCK

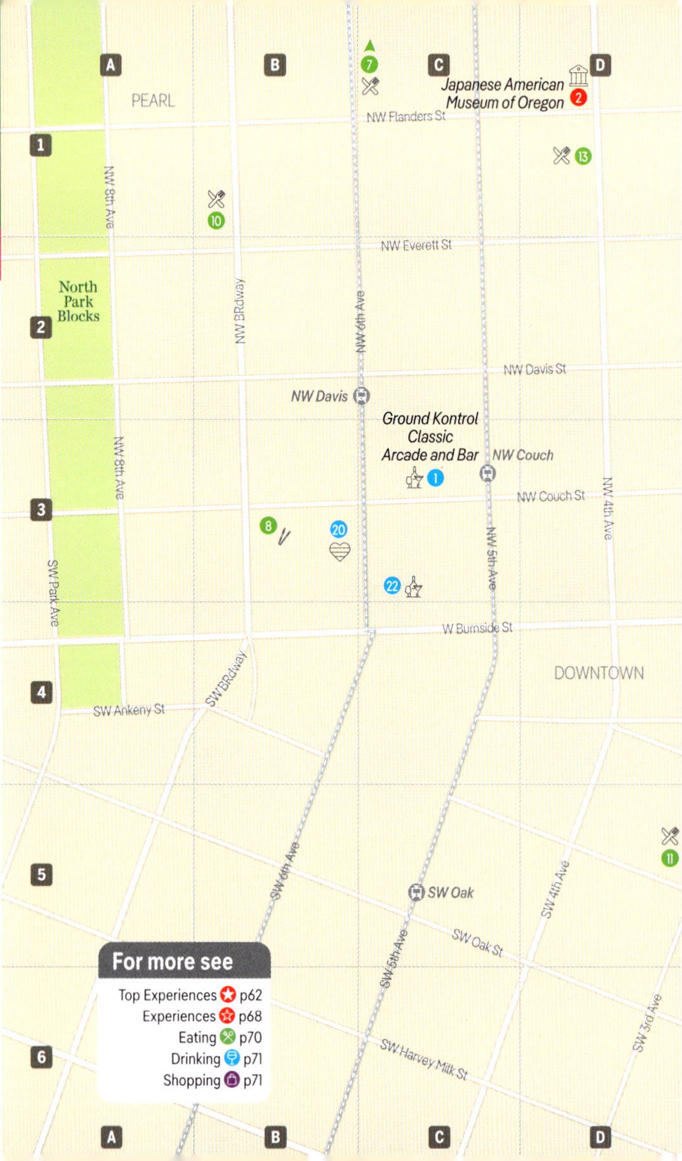

A B C D

PEARL

Japanese American Museum of Oregon 2

NW Flanders St

7

13

10

NW 8th Ave

NW Everett St

North Park Blocks

NW BRdway

NW 6th Ave

NW Davis St

NW Davis

Ground Kontrol Classic Arcade and Bar 1

NW Couch

NW Couch St

NW 4th Ave

8

20

NW 5th Ave

22

SW Park Ave

W Burnside St

DOWNTOWN

SW BRdway

SW Ankeny St

11

SW 6th Ave

SW Oak

SW 4th Ave

SW Oak St

SW 5th Ave

SW 3rd Ave

SW Harvey Milk St

1 2 3 4 5 6

For more see
Top Experiences p62
Experiences p68
Eating p70
Drinking p71
Shopping p71

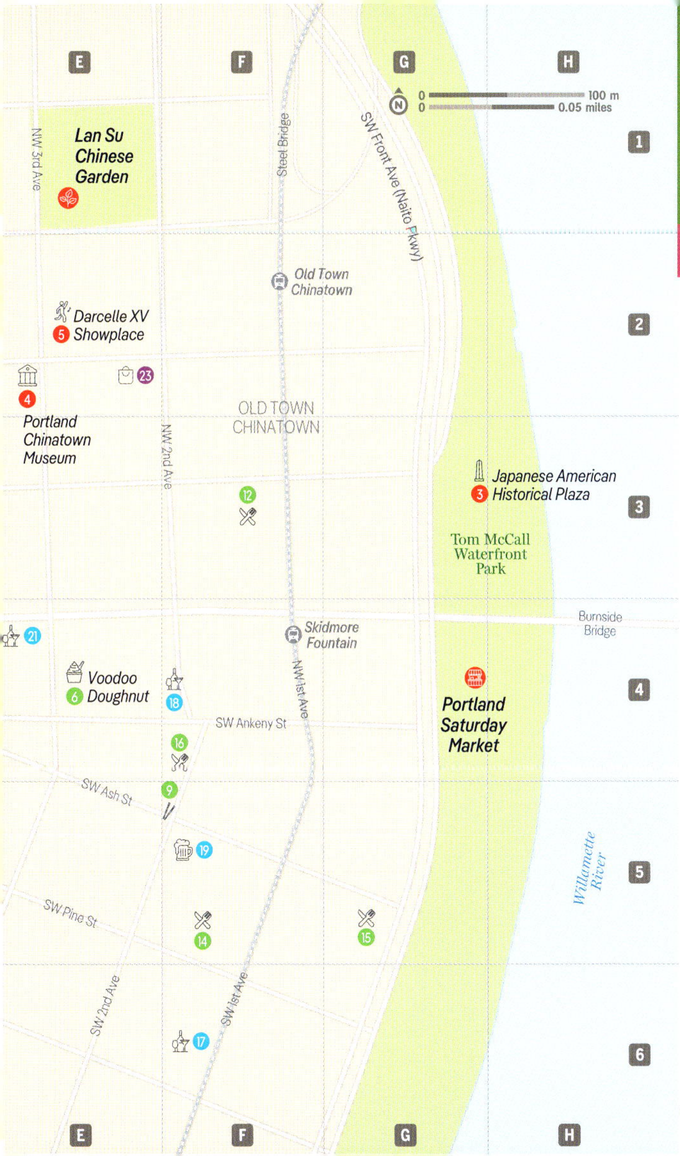

E F G H

0 100 m
0 0.05 miles

1 2 3 4 5 6

Lan Su Chinese Garden

NW 3rd Ave

Steel Bridge

SW Front Ave (Naito Pkwy)

Old Town Chinatown

5 Darcelle XV Showplace

23

4 Portland Chinatown Museum

OLD TOWN CHINATOWN

NW 2nd Ave

12

3 Japanese American Historical Plaza

Tom McCall Waterfront Park

Burnside Bridge

21

Skidmore Fountain

NW 1st Ave

6 Voodoo Doughnut

18

Portland Saturday Market

SW Ankeny St

16

9

SW Ash St

19

Willamette River

SW Pine St

14

15

SW 2nd Ave

SW 1st Ave

17

★ TOP EXPERIENCE

Portland Saturday Market

Sine 1974, Portland's craftiest artisans have been selling their wares at the Portland Saturday Market, the largest continuously operating open-air craft market in the US. Here you'll find everything from handcrafted jewelry to colorful apparel, not to mention loads of food carts and live entertainment.

MAP P61 **G4**

PLANNING TIPS
Arrive early in the morning to avoid crowds. Most vendors take credit cards and/or digital payment. But carry cash, just in case.

Getting Crafty

The market extends from the 19th-century **Skidmore Fountain** on SW 1st and Ankeny down to a stretch of Waterfront Park, under, and just south of, the Burnside Bridge. Here you'll find over 150 vendors selling housewares, clothes and art prints.

The market operates on Saturdays from March until Christmas Eve, and is open daily during the week before Christmas, for a special event known as the **Festival of the Last Minute**. Many artisans keep their booths for many years, but there are usually plenty of new vendors every season.

Unlike many markets, everything sold at the Portland Saturday Market must be handcrafted by the booth's owner, so you're likely to be purchasing your products from the person who made them.

Portland Skidmore Market

On the opposite (west) side of the Skidmore Fountain, the Portland Skidmore Market is often viewed as an extension of the Saturday Market, but it's actually its own entity. It hosts a mix of product vendors and food carts, but unlike the Saturday Market, the Skidmore Market allows vendors to sell items that they didn't craft themselves. While you'll still see plenty of booths selling

Scan for information.

QUIGGYT4/SHUTTERSTOCK

handmade wares on the Skidmore Market side, you'll also find plenty of more eclectic offerings, including housewares and clothes imported from Guatemala, Nepal and beyond.

Beyond Shopping

Most people visit the Saturday and Skidmore markets to pick up gifts and souvenirs, but it's also a great place to stop for a bite or to watch live entertainment. There's a stretch of food trucks specializing in everything from pizza to pretzels. Some vendors – including **Horn of Africa**, which serves East African fare – have had a presence at the market for generations. It's worth bringing your lunch to the main stage, where music performances often run from late morning well into the afternoon.

QUICK BREAK
Fuel up with an elephant ear (also known as 'fried dough') at **PDX Original Elephant Ears**. They're best served with copious amounts of sugar and cinnamon.

★ TOP EXPERIENCE

Lan Su Chinese Garden

Spread out over 40,000 sq ft in the heart of Old Town Chinatown, Lan Su Chinese Garden feels like it's worlds away. It was designed to mimic a traditional scholar's garden and features a mix of Ming Dynasty–style architectural elements, foliage and ponds.

MAP P61 **E1**

PLANNING TIP
Download the free Discover Lan Su app for access to additional garden info, audio tours and a family-friendly mobile scavenger hunt.

Scan for information.

The Backstory

Considered one of the finest examples of a traditional Chinese garden design in the US, Lan Su opened its doors in 2000. The seed was planted in 1988, however, when the city of Suzhou in China became Portland's sister city. Construction started a decade later, when dozens of artisans from Suzhou came to Portland to begin work on the garden, using materials sourced from their hometown. Although the garden is a modern creation, it's largely inspired by garden architecture from the Ming Dynasty (1368–1644 CE).

Garden Features

The garden is characterized by a series of interconnected walkways that wrap around a large central pond, passing through covered pavilions and a mix of indoor workshop spaces and outdoor gardens. Visitors enter through the **Courtyard of Tranquility**, a buffer zone between the bustle of Old Town and the calm of the garden, passing through the lattice-crowned **Hall of Brocade Clouds** (which also hosts a gift shop) and into the garden itself. Highlights include the **Moon Locking Pavilion**, accessible via a walkway that juts into the middle of the pond, and the **Tower of Cosmic Reflections**, a gorgeous double-story

JON BILOUS/SHUTTERSTOCK

structure adorned with intricate woodwork that houses Lan Su's tea room.

Cultural Experiences

Along with a solid schedule of seasonal events, Lan Su includes plenty of weekly cultural experiences with admission. These include calligraphy demonstrations held by expert calligrapher Wang Xing, Chinese conversation workshops led by native speakers and live-music performances that showcase traditional Chinese instruments. You can also learn the fundamentals of tai chi and qigong or learn how to play Weiqi – a checkers-like board game also known as Go. While most of these activities only take place between spring and fall, the garden does offer plant-focused lectures every Wednesday, throughout the year.

QUICK BREAK

It's worth stopping on-site for a cuppa at the two-story **Yun Shui Teahouse**, a beautiful tea room with garden views and a large tea and treat menu.

Walk Old Town Chinatown

A walk through Old Town Chinatown is a great way to learn about the neighborhood and the Asian American communities that lived here in Portland's early days. This tour takes half an hour if you just walk from point to point, but it's worth slowing down to visit the museums, gardens and, perhaps, grab a donut.

START	END	LENGTH
Chinatown Gateway	Voodoo Doughnut	1 mile; 30 minutes

1 Beyond the Gate

There's no better place to begin your walk through Old Town Chinatown than at the **Chinatown Gateway**, an ornate entry arch that crowns NW 4th Ave at Burnside St. Give yourself time to admire the arch's colorful dragon designs and the duo of bronze lions that flank the three-tiered entry before heading into Chinatown.

2 Living History

Continue along 4th Ave for another two blocks, passing by the neighborhood's beloved (and snicker-worthy) Hung Far Low sign, all that remains of what was once one of Chinatown's most beloved restaurants. Walk for another block to the **Portland Chinatown Museum**, which tells the story of the Chinese American community that shaped the neighborhood.

3 Garden of Delights

Your next destination is **Lan Su Chinese Garden**, an impeccable Ming Dynasty–style garden tucked among the neighborhood's mix of 19th-century stone edifices and drab parking lots. You can't see much of it from the outside, but if you opt not to stop en route, it's worth returning for a couple of hours to explore the interior.

4 Japantown

Despite Chinatown's name, part of the neighborhood also once had a large Japanese community. Learn about some of Portland's – and Oregon's – early Japanese American residents at the **Japanese American Museum of Oregon**.

5 History in Bloom

After visiting the museum, head west toward Governor Tom McCall Waterfront Park to check out the **Japanese American Historical Plaza**, which honors the Japanese Americans who were interned in WWII prison camps in Oregon. If you visit during the early spring, you might get to see the hundred cherry trees that line the plaza in full bloom.

6 Arts & Crafts

If you visit on a Saturday, make sure to stop at the **Portland Saturday Market** (p62), a massive craft market that's been running since the mid-1970s. Expect plenty of tie-dye, along with food carts, live music and local art.

7 Sweet Stop

Finish your walk with a stop at Portland's most famous dessert destination: **Voodoo Doughnut** (p69). While the jury's out on whether the doughnuts here are the best in the city, they certainly are the weirdest. Try the Voodoo Doll doughnut, which is shaped like a human and filled with a gush of blood-red jelly.

EXPERIENCES

Try Your Luck at Ground Kontrol Classic Arcade and Bar ARCADE

MAP: 1 P60 C3

Get in touch with your inner video-game-obsessed child at **Ground Kontrol Classic Arcade and Bar** *(groundkontrol.com)*, which features two floors of video games and pinball machines, including plenty of vintage favorites dating as far back as the 1970s (think Ms Pac-Man, Tetris and even Frogger). Regular pinball competitions and free-flowing beer keep the environment lively in the evenings. Kids under 21 are welcome to join in the fun as long as they leave by 5pm.

Learn about Japanese History MUSEUM

Not many people know that Portland had its own Japantown within Chinatown. A small section of the neighborhood, also known by its Japanese name, Nihonmachi, had a substantial Japanese American population from the late 1800s well into the 20th century. You can learn the story of Oregon's early Japanese residents with a visit to the **Japanese American Museum of Oregon** (MAP: 2 P60 D1; *jamo.org; adult/youth/child $8/5/free)*. From here, it's a 10-minute walk to the **Japanese American Historical Plaza** (MAP: 3 P61 G3; *free)* at Waterfront Park, which honors the Japanese Americans who were held in internment camps during WWII, in a clear violation of the Bill of Rights. The plaza features 12 granite stones that feature poetry by Japanese American poets, while a 13th stone bears the names of the internment camps. Docents lead tours of the plaza with advance reservation; self-guided tours narrated by George Takei are also available by downloading the Public Art PDX iPhone app.

Step Back in Time at the Portland Chinatown Museum MUSEUM

MAP: 4 P61 E2

The best place to learn about Chinatown's roots, and the Chinese American experience in Oregon in general, is at the **Portland Chinatown Museum** *(portlandchinatownmuseum.org; adult/youth/child $8/5/free)*. The permanent exhibit, Beyond the Gate: A Tale of Portland's Historic Chinatowns, is reason enough to visit, and does a fantastic job of chronicling the rise of Chinatown through a mix of photos, interpretive panels and ephemera from some of the neighborhood's earliest residents. There's also a life-size recreation of a section of the Hung Far Low Restaurant, a no-longer-operating restaurant that was once among Chinatown's most popular places to eat. The museum also hosts a number of events, including an annual **Dragon Dance Parade** in honor of Chinese New Year.

Watch the Drag Queens Work It at Darcelle XV Showplace

DRAG CABARET

MAP: 5 P61 E2

Opened in 1967 by Walter Willard Cole, an LGBTIQ+ activist and artist best known for his drag persona, Darcelle, **Darcelle XV Showplace** *(darcellexv.com)* is among Old Town's most important cultural institutions. Cole – who was deemed the oldest drag performer on earth by Guinness World Records – passed away in 2023. Still, the queens at the Showplace continue to carry the torch, with Vegas-style revue performances every Friday and Saturday night and again on Sundays at brunch. If you get a chance, try to attend a performance hosted by Poison Waters, a Portland cultural icon in her own right.

VOODOO DOUGHNUT

Spend much time in Old Town Chinatown and you're likely to see people carrying large pink cake boxes around with them. What's inside is not cake, but doughnuts from the city's acclaimed Voodoo Doughnut. This local establishment shot to fame in the early oughts because of its unusual concoctions, which ended up getting it in a bit of trouble (think doughnuts laced with NyQuil). Although the flavors are tamer these days, visitors continue to flock to Voodoo's flagship Old Town location to buy boxes of doughnuts designed to resemble voodoo dolls and pentagrams. Be prepared for long lines on weekends.

MAP: 6 P61 E4

THE SHANGHAI TUNNELS

According to local lore, there's a network of subterranean passageways that lead from the historic saloons and hotels of Old Town to the banks of the Willamette River. Legend has it that these tunnels – known as the Shanghai Tunnels – were once used as part of an elaborate scheme in which drunk men would be kidnapped from local establishments and smuggled to ships to work as enslaved sailors. While there's little evidence to back up these claims, some tour operators bring guests to local basements on so-called Shanghai Tunnel tours.

Best Places for...

See p60 for map of locations

$ Budget $$ Midrange $$$ Top End

Eating

American

Wilf's Restaurant & Jazz Bar $$$
 C1
Creole classics meet Pacific Northwest ingredients at this snazzy spot in Union Station. White tablecloths, an extensive wine list and live jazz most nights add extra oomph to the ambience. *wilfsrestaurant.com; 5-9pm Wed-Sat, 5-9:30pm Fri & Sat*

Asian

Sushi Ichiban $
 B3
Fill up on fresh (and reasonably priced) rolls straight from a sushi train at this beloved hole-in-the-wall dinner spot. *instagram.com/official_sushi_ichiban; 4-9pm Wed-Sun*

Xin Ding Dumpling House $$
 F5
Order dim sum, noodles, hot pot and more at this popular spot, housed in a converted Chinatown pub. *xindingdumplinghouse.com; hours vary*

Breakfast

John's Cafe $
10 B1
Feast on pancakes, eggs and French toast at this diner-style breakfast spot that's been keeping Portlanders satiated for generations. *7am-1:30pm Mon-Sat*

Kingsland Kitchen $$
 D5
Mix scrambles, briskets and benedicts with mimosas and hair-of-the-dog cocktails at this self-appointed brunch club. *kingslandkitchen.com; 9am-2pm Thu-Tue*

Coffee

Café United $
 F3
Pair hot tea and espresso drinks with bagels, sandwiches and nachos at this Black-owned coffee shop featuring exposed brick walls both indoors and in an airy courtyard. *facebook.com/oldtowncoffeepdx; hours vary Wed-Sun*

Monte Rossa Cafe $
 D1
Stop by this family-owned coffee shop and delicatessen for classic coffee drinks, tasty breakfast pastries and hearty sandwiches. *instagram.com/monterossacafe; 8am-3pm Mon-Fri*

Food Hall

Pine Street Market $$
14 F5
Choose your own culinary adventure at this gourmet food hall, which is anchored by local favorites such as Matsunoki Ramen and the Pine Street Taproom. *pinestreetpdx.com; 11am-9pm*

Latin American

Lechon $$$
 G5
Stop in for happy hour or treat yourself to a dinner of South American–

inspired dishes ranging from *lomo saltado* to Argentine-style steak at this spot across from the waterfront. *lechonpdx.com; 4-9pm Mon-Thu, to 10pm Fri & Sat*

Seafood

Dan & Louis Oyster Bar $$

This classic spot has been operating since 1907, making it almost as old as Old Town itself. It has been owned by the same family for five generations. *danandlouis.com; noon-9pm Fri-Mon*

Drinking

Bars

Raven's Manor

17 F6

Immerse yourself in the spooky world of ghoulish cocktails and eerie desserts at this Gothed-out theme bar inspired by a haunted mansion. *ravensmanorexperience.com; 5-11pm Wed-Mon, to midnight Fri & Sat*

Shanghai Tunnel Bar

18 F4

Head underground for a laid-back evening of pool, pinball, cocktails and tasty noodle bowls at this subterranean Old Town favorite. *instagram.com/shanghaitunnelbar; 5pm-2am Wed-Mon, from noon Sat*

Irish Pub

Kell's Irish Pub

19 F5

Pair whiskey and Guinness with shepherd's pie or sausage rolls at this longstanding spot, where it's always St Patrick's Day. *kellsportland.com; 4-10pm Wed & Thu, noon-midnight Fri & Sat*

LGBTIQ+

Silverado

One of the oldest and largest gay men's bars in Oregon, this spot has male strippers and a dance floor downstairs and a more bar-like experience upstairs, with video poker and pool. *silveradopdx.com; 9am-2:30am*

Live Music

Dante's

21 E4

This gritty spot on West Burnside features live entertainment on most nights that ranges from heavy-metal bands to karaoke. Come on a Sunday for the Sinferno Cabaret, which features fire dancing, loud music and tatted-up performers. *danteslive.com; 11am-2:30am*

Roseland Theater

22 C3

If the walls at this longstanding all-ages music venue could talk, they'd tell you about the serious roster of musicians who've played here over the years, from rock and reggae stars to internationally renowned electronic-music producers. *roselandpdx.com*

Shopping

Snacks

Goodies Snack Shop

23 E2

Pick up sweets, soft drinks and savory snacks from around the world – as well as treats for your face made by popular Korean beauty brands – at this eclectic treat spot. *goodiessnackshop.com; 11am-6pm Tue-Fri, to 5pm Sat & Sun*

See p85
for eating, drinking and shopping listings

Researched by Margot Bigg

Explore Northwest Portland & Pearl District

While most Portland shopping areas have a hipster vibe, that's far from the case in Northwest Portland and its Pearl District, where the atmosphere is decidedly upscale. The Pearl District is best described as industrial-chic, consisting of a mix of old warehouses that were revamped into loft condos and chichi storefronts. It's also home to Powell's City of Books, which has been drawing bibliophiles to the area since the 1970s. The rest of Northwest Portland, particularly the areas around NW 21st and NW 23rd Aves (known both as 'Nob Hill' and the 'Alphabet District'), is dominated by quintessentially Portland red-brick structures and stately Victorian mansions.

Getting Around

Streetcar

The A and B Loops and the North-South Lines of the Portland Streetcar stop in the Pearl District. The North-South Line continues to Nob Hill up NW Lovejoy St, all the way up to NW 23rd Ave, before turning around and heading back toward downtown via NW Northrup St.

Bus

Bus route 20 runs east to west along Burnside St on both sides of the river. Bus route 15 runs from Belmont St in SE Portland, through downtown and up to Nob Hill.

THE BEST

BOOKSTORE Powell's City of Books (p76)

URBAN WOODLAND Forest Park (p78)

ART EXPERIENCE First Thursday Street Gallery (p81)

STATELY HOME Pittock Mansion (p82)

WEIRD WONDER Freakybuttrue Peculiarium (p82)

Freakybuttrue Peculiarium (p82)
ZUMA PRESS, INC./ALAMY

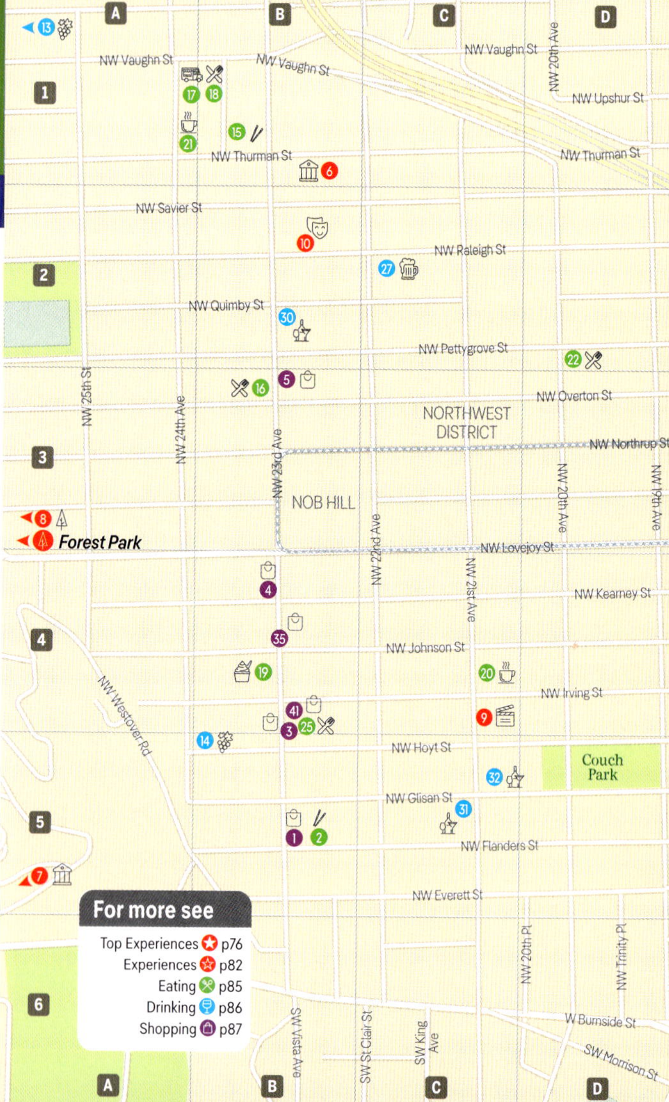
A
B
C
D
1
2
3
4
5
6
NW Vaughn St
NW Vaughn St
NW Vaughn St
NW 20th Ave
NW Upshur St
NW Thurman St
NW Thurman St
NW Savier St
NW Raleigh St
NW Quimby St
NW Pettygrove St
NW Overton St
NORTHWEST DISTRICT
NW Northrup St
NW 25th St
NW 24th Ave
NW 23rd Ave
NOB HILL
NW 22nd Ave
NW 20th Ave
NW 19th Ave
Forest Park
NW Lovejoy St
NW 21st Ave
NW Kearney St
NW Johnson St
NW Westover Rd
NW Irving St
NW Hoyt St
Couch Park
NW Glisan St
NW Flanders St
NW Everett St
NW 20th Pl
NW Trinity Pl
SW Vista Ave
SW St Clair St
SW King Ave
W Burnside St
SW Morrison St
For more see
Top Experiences p76
Experiences p82
Eating p85
Drinking p86
Shopping p87

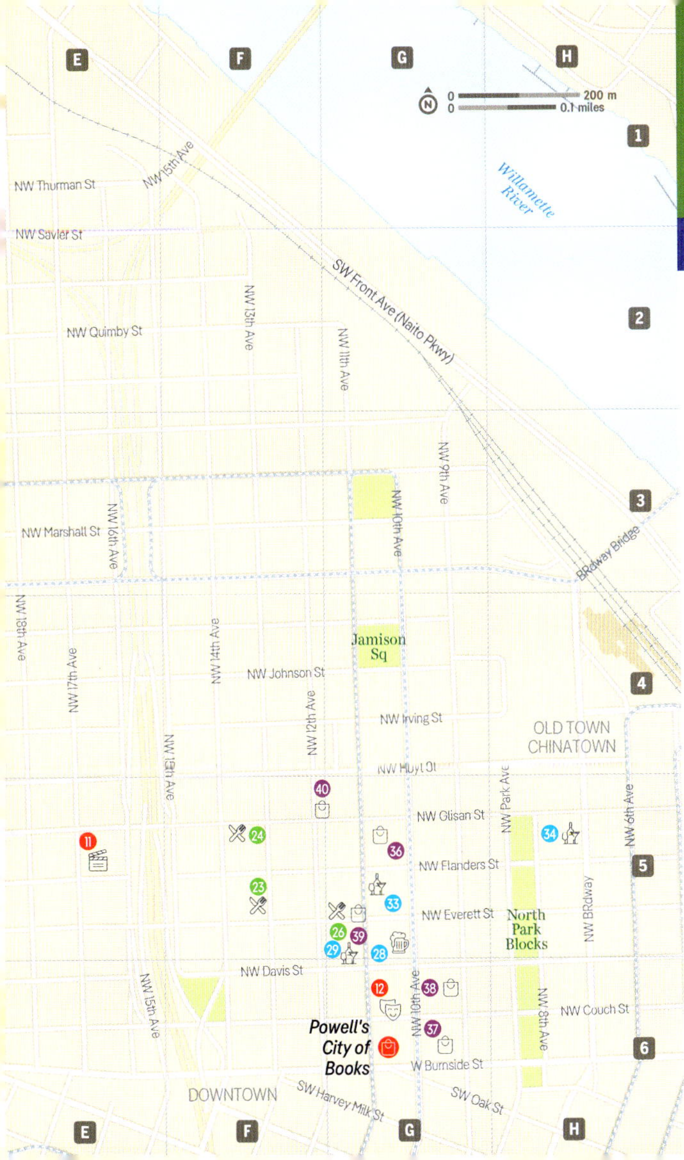

E F G H

0 200 m
0 0.1 miles

1 2 3 4 5 6

Willamette River

NW Thurman St
NW 15th Ave
NW Savier St
SW Front Ave (Naito Pkwy)
NW 13th Ave
NW 11th Ave
NW Quimby St
NW 9th Ave
NW 10th Ave
NW Marshall St
NW 16th Ave
BRdway Bridge
NW 18th Ave
NW 17th Ave
NW 14th Ave
Jamison Sq
NW Johnson St
NW 12th Ave
NW Irving St
OLD TOWN CHINATOWN
NW 13th Ave
NW Hoyt St
NW Park Ave
NW Glisan St
NW 6th Ave
NW Flanders St
NW BRdway
NW Everett St
North Park Blocks
NW Davis St
NW 15th Ave
NW 10th Ave
NW 8th Ave
NW Couch St
Powell's City of Books
W Burnside St
DOWNTOWN
SW Harvey Milk St
SW Oak St

11 12 23 24 26 28 29 33 34 36 37 38 39 40

E F G H

★ TOP EXPERIENCE

Powell's City of Books

Portland's most famous bookstore, Powell's City of Books, is also one of the city's major draws, especially for die-hard bibliophiles. Spread out over three floors and an entire city block, this massive store touts itself as the world's largest new and used independent bookshop on earth.

MAP P75 **G6**

PLANNING TIP
The parking structure at Powell's is small and cramped. If you have a larger vehicle, park on the street or at the nearby Whole Foods.

Scan for information.

A City of Books

Powell's has over a million books in stock at any given time, which can be as overwhelming as it is intriguing. To make finding your way around easier, Powell's is divided into different rooms, each with a color theme. Rooms are further broken down into category. You will still need a store map, however, especially if there are specific sections you don't want to miss. Printed maps are available online and at both of the two store entrances (at NW 10th Ave and Burnside and at NW 11th and Couch). Each room has at least one staffed information counter plus a computer or two where you can search for books by title or author.

All books at Powell's are displayed together, which means you won't find different sections for new and used books. Prices of used books can vary quite a bit, so if you find multiple used copies of the same book, make sure to check the pricing. Lower-priced books often have underlined text or some damage, however, so it's best to double check the pages if you find a serious bargain.

The Rare Book Room

Serious collectors and those looking for beautifully bound antiquarian books shouldn't miss the Rare Book Room, which houses thousands of hard-to-

DAVID BUZZARD/SHUTTERSTOCK

find titles, as well as autographed works and 1st editions. For an added dose of charm, the room is designed to resemble an old library, complete with dark-wood bookshelves, antique furniture and soft lighting. The space only allows 14 customers at a time; to access it, head to the Pearl Room information counter on the 3rd floor and ask for a pass.

Other Branches

As well as the flagship store, you'll find Powell's around town too. The second-largest store is in the suburb city of Beaverton, in a large (and very un-Portland) outdoor shopping center. There's also a charming location over on SE Hawthorne Blvd and a small branch at the Portland International Airport, in the South Concourse, just past security.

QUICK BREAK
Curl up with a book from Powell's at **Guilder Cafe**, a coffeeshop inside the bookstore. Pastries, sandwiches and cocktails are on the menu.

★ TOP EXPERIENCE

Forest Park

You don't need to rent a car to experience the majesty of an Oregon forest. Simply head to Forest Park, a 5200-acre expanse of trails and trees that sits just beyond Northwest Portland's Nob Hill neighborhood.

PLANNING TIP
Pick up the *Forest Park Trail Map and Visitor's Guide* at Powell's City of Books or the Forest Park Conservancy office (833 SW 11th Ave, Suite 800) before you set out.

Scan for information.

The Wildwood Trail

Forest Park has over 80 miles of trails that attract plenty of runners and hikers, especially on sunny days. The longest is the Wildwood Trail, a 30.2-mile path that runs from Newberry Rd at the northernmost end of the park clear down to Washington Park. Although this designated National Recreation Trail is undoubtedly long, it's not particularly challenging, and it lacks some of the ultra-steep ascents you'll find in wilder parts of Oregon. Still, most people opt to hike it in segments rather than attempting to do the whole trail in one go.

Other Great Trails

A favorite among runners and cyclists, **Leif Erikson Drive** is a former road that is now closed to traffic. It stretches from the end of NW Thurman St near Aspen Ave for 11 miles to NW Germantown Rd, crossing many other trails along the way.

For a shorter jaunt, head to **Lower Macleay Park** *(2960 NW Upshur St)*, the trailhead of the 0.8-mile **Lower Macleay Trail**. This leads from the park to a stone structure known as the Witch's Castle, passing under a canopy of big-leaf maple, western red cedar and moss-covered Douglas fir trees that stretch as far as the eye can see. From

JARED STINE/SHUTTERSTOCK

the castle, you can continue for around 1.7 miles up the Wildwood Trail to the Pittock Mansion (p82), a stately old home that happens to have some of the best views in the city.

Witch's Castle

Although Forest Park's signposts may point you in the direction of a 'Stone House,' the abandoned stone shelter at the base of the Wildwood Trail is best known by its more intriguing moniker: Witch's Castle (pictured). Built in 1929, the shelter once housed a tool room, a picnic shelter and what were, at the time, Portland's most remote public restrooms. It was decommissioned in 1964 and is now mostly used as a spot for hikers to take selfies – and for local teens to get into mischief.

QUICK BREAK
Fuel up with a coffee and a pastry at **Haven Coffee Co** on NW 28th and Thurman, a five-minute walk from Lower Macleay Park.

WALKING TOUR

Walk the Pearl District

While the Pearl District is a great place for window-shopping and restaurant-hopping, it's the famous galleries that make for the best stops. The best time to do this gallery walk is on the first Thursday of the month, when galleries stay open late and a stretch of road is transformed into an outdoor art exhibit.

START	END	LENGTH
Blue Sky, Oregon Center for the Photographic Arts	First Thursday Street Gallery	0.8 miles; 30 minutes

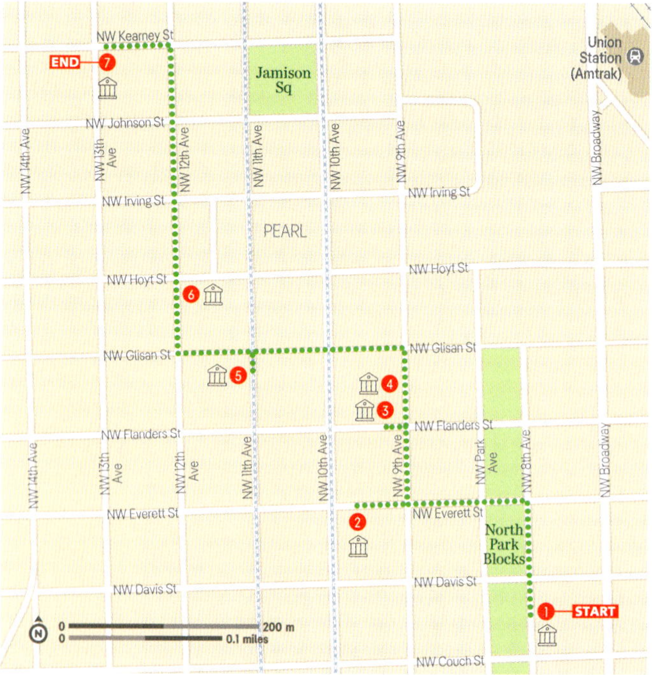

1 Picture Perfect

Start your walk at Portland's foremost photography gallery, **Blue Sky, Oregon Center for the Photographic Arts**. Blue Sky started back in the 1970s as a photography collective, and one of its former locations was among the Pearl District's pioneering galleries back when the area was first becoming an art hub in the 1980s.

2 Cooperative Creativity

Head north along the North Park Blocks and hang a left on Everett St. After a couple of blocks, you'll reach **Blackfish Gallery**, another old-school Pearl District institution. Established as an artist cooperative in 1978, over the decades since this multi-space gallery has showcased the works of over 200 major artists from the Pacific Northwest.

3 Emerging Artists

Continue north for a block until you reach one of the newer additions to Portland's contemporary art scene: **ILY2** (the name is an acronym for 'I Love You Too'). The space showcases the works of early- and mid-career artists through a feminist lens.

4 Art Establishment

Just next door to the new kid on the block is one of the oldest galleries in the Pearl District: the **Elizabeth Leach Gallery**. It was established in 1981 by the daughter of business mogul Howard H Leach, and has represented some of the Pacific Northwest's most acclaimed artists in the decades that have followed.

5 Community Connections

Continue past industrial buildings that have been repurposed into swanky loft condos and shiny storefronts for another couple of blocks to **Gallery 114**, an artist-operated collective that has been showcasing works across media since opening back in 1990. Exhibits feature works of both coop members and guest artists.

6 Art Therapy

It's only two blocks to your next stop, the **J Pepin Art Gallery**, a contemporary art gallery with a cause: 'reframing the perception of mental illness to be one of mental health.' Artists represented here are encouraged to share their own journeys with mental health alongside their works.

7 Art for All

Not all of the art in the Pearl District is found within the walls of the area's acclaimed galleries. Browse the works of budding artists at the **First Thursday Street Gallery**, an open-air gallery that takes over three blocks of NW 13th Ave, between Hoyt and Kearney Sts, on the first Thursday of the month from April to October, between 5pm and 9pm.

EXPERIENCES

Stroll Through Nob Hill in Alphabetical Order SHOPPING

Affectionately nicknamed the 'Alphabet District' because its street names are in alphabetical order from south to north, Nob Hill offers some of the best boutique shopping in town, especially along NW 23rd Ave. A good place to start is on the corner of NW 23rd and Flanders to visit **Snow Peak** (MAP: 1 P74 **B5**; *snowpeak.com*), the US flagship location of the beloved Japanese outdoor gear and apparel brand. Inside, you'll find everything from titanium chopsticks (and sporks!) to foldable fire pits. Snow Peak also has its own restaurant, **Takibi** (MAP: 2 P74 **B5**; *takibipdx.com*), which serves up tasty ramen and Japanese snacks. From here, head north down NW 23rd toward NW Hoyt, where you'll find funky women's boutique **Ipnosi** (MAP: 3 P74 **B4**; *ipnosiclothing.com*) next door to pet accessory store **Hip Hound** (*hiphoundshop.com*). Parents with young kids shouldn't miss the oversized stuffed animals at **Mud-Puddles Toys & Books** (MAP: 4 P74 **B4**; *mudpuddlestoys.com*) on NW Kearney, while travelers interested in spirituality and crystals will want to give themselves at least an hour to browse the shelves at **New Renaissance Bookstore** (MAP: 5 P74 **B3**; *newrenbooks.com*) on NW 23rd and Pettygrove.

Fly Your Freak Flag at Freakybuttrue Peculiarium MUSEUM

MAP: 6 P74 **B1**

Portland prides itself in celebrating the weird, which is surely part of the secret to the success of **Freakybuttrue Peculiarium** (*peculiarium.com; Wednesday to Monday $10, Tuesday $7*). Despite being located in one of the posher parts of town, this museum-shop hybrid draws in fun-loving folks with its zany collection of oddities, many of which are for sale. With 15 minutes at this weird little museum, you'll be able to see an alien autopsy, horror-inspired miniature displays and – if you're lucky – Bigfoot himself. Come in costume (or bring a pet along) and they'll let you in for free.

Visit the Past at the Pittock Mansion HISTORIC HOME

MAP: 7 P74 **A5**

Skirting the edge of Forest Park, **Pittock Mansion** (*pittockmasion.org; adult/child $15.50/11.50*) offers a glimpse into what life in Portland was like for ultra-rich residents at the turn of the 20th century. This 23-room mansion was built by Henry Pittock, a timber baron and one of the first publishers of the *Oregonian* newspaper. Today it's run as a museum, inviting visitors to roam its bedrooms, sleeping porches and lounges, all decorated with elegant period furnishings and original art and ephemera. If you don't want to pay to go inside, you can explore the 46-acre estate's gardens free of charge and take in spectacular views of the city below. While you can drive to the mansion, many visitors prefer to come on foot, hiking up to the house via Forest Park's Wildwood Trail (p78).

Spread Your Wings Bird Alliance of Oregon
NATURE

On the edge of Forest Park, the **Bird Alliance of Oregon** (MAP: 8 P74 **B4**; *birdallianceoregon.org; free*), formerly known as the Portland Audubon Society, is a great place to learn about birds while getting your steps in. This 172-acre wooded sanctuary has an interpretive center with bird-focused exhibits, enclosures where you can visit ambassador animals (including Bybee the turtle and Julio the great horned owl) and a 4-mile network of trails. At the end of your visit, stop by the **Nature Store** and support the Bird Alliance by purchasing birding gear and books.

BEST ENTERTAINMENT OPTIONS IN NW & THE PEARL

Cinema 21
An art-house movie theater on NW 21st Ave that specializes in independent and foreign films.
MAP: 9 P74 **C4**

CoHo Theatre
A playhouse that stages works by CoHo Productions, Third Rail Repertory Theatre and the Portland Experimental Theatre Ensemble.
MAP: 10 P74 **B2**

McMenamins Mission Theater
A 1912 Swedish Evangelical Mission Covenant Church turned theater with live music and lectures, plus a pub.
MAP: 11 P74 **E5**

Portland Center Stage at the Armory
A Victorian-era armory-turned-performing arts venue with 190- and 590-seat theaters.
MAP: 12 P75 **G6**

SIMPSONSPIRATION

Spend much time strolling around Northwest Portland and you're sure to notice some familiar names, at least if you're a fan of the animated TV series *The Simpsons*. The cartoon's creator, Matt Groening, is from Portland and many of his characters share their names with Portland streets. There's Flanders St, the inspiration for the name Ned Flanders (a pedestrian bridge named after the neighborly character runs from NW 14th to 15th Aves) or Kearney St, which lends its name to the show's school bully. The program's preacher, Reverend Lovejoy, shares his surname with Lovejoy St (which is named for Asa Lovejoy, one of Portland's founders).

Go Urban Wine Tasting

WINE

You don't have to drive all the way to the Willamette Valley to get the Oregon wine-tasting experience. You just need to make your way to **Boedecker Cellars** (MAP: 13 P74 A1; *boedeckercellars.com; tastings $25;* pictured) in the Northwest Industrial District, just north of Nob Hill. This family-run urban winery in a refurbished mid-century warehouse serves its most popular wines, most of which are pinot noir or chardonnay, by the glass and by the flight, in a tasting space lined with massive oak barrels or outdoors on a pet-friendly patio.

To try a solid range of wines representing some of the Pacific Northwest's most lauded viticultural regions, head to **Fossil & Fawn** (MAP: 14 P74 B5; *fossilandfawn.com; tastings $30)* in Nob Hill, where you can enjoy a guided tasting led by winemaker-owners Jenny and Jim. You'll need to make reservations to access the space, however, as tastings take place in the owners' residence/workspace, speakeasy style. Must-tries include an orange wine-inspired dewürztraminer and pinot blanc blend and naturally sparkling Pét Nat produced with Willamette Valley grapes.

JAI SOOTS/BOEDECKER CELLARS

Best Places for...

$ Budget $$ Midrange $$$ Top End

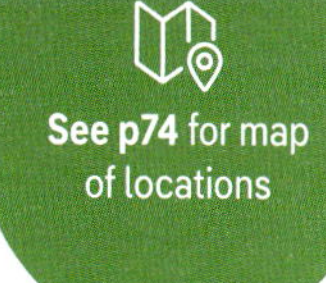

Eating

Asian

Langbaan $$$

 B1

This miniature Nob Hill restaurant with only 24 seats offers set Thai tasting menus that rely on seasonal ingredients and optional wine pairings. *langbaanportland.com; 5:30-8:15pm Wed-Sun*

Top Burmese Burma Joy $$

 B3

Adorable robot servers deliver heaping plates of noodles and tea-leaf salads to diners at this casual Burmese spot in Nob Hill (don't worry, there are humans who work here, too). *topburmese.com; 11:30am-9pm*

Village Kitchen $

 A1

Located in the Nob Hill Food Cart Pod, this little spot serves tasty Burmese and fusion fare, with dishes that range from tea-leaf salad in a hot-and-sour sauce to reimagined macaroni and cheese with a Southeast Asian touch. *villagekitchenpdx.com; noon-8pm Tue-Sun*

American

Farmer and the Beast $

 B1

Enjoy smash burgers, seasonal salads and crinkle-cut fries at this no-frills Slabtown food cart that sources ingredients from local farms. *instagram.com/farmerandthebeast; 11:30am-8pm Wed-Sun*

Papa Haydn $$$

 D4

This chic restaurant serves French-inspired salads and sandwiches along with steak and pasta, but it's the rich cakes and other desserts that have earned this Portland classic a cult following among sweet tooths. *papahaydn.com/pages/nw-portland; 11:30am-10pm*

Coffee

Coffee Time $

 C4

If you're looking for a place to curl up with a good book, this long-standing coffeehouse with multiple nooks and rooms is a great option. *coffeetimepdx.com; 7am-6pm*

Dragonfly Coffee House $

 A1

This adorable community coffee shop in Nob Hill serves tasty pastries, tea and espresso drinks, plus a small selection of European wines and Oregon beers. *thedragonflycoffeehouse.com; 7am-5pm Sat-Thu, to 7pm Fri*

Mediterranean

Gastro Mania Deli NW $$

 D2

Don't let the less-than-appetizing name put you off of this funky gyro spot, which serves innovative takes on traditional Mediterranean fare (think breakfast gyros and bacon-wrapped dolmas). *gastromania24.com; 8:30am-6pm Mon-Sat, 9am-5pm Sun*

Mediterranean Exploration Company $$

23 F5

Flavors from Greece and the Levant are showcased at this Pearl District spot, which offers a huge outdoor seating area that gets busy on summer evenings. *sesamecollective.com/mec; 4-10pm*

Peruvian

Andina $$$

 F5

Enjoy seasonally inspired Peruvian classics with a Pacific Northwest twist and tasty cocktails (pisco sours, anyone?) at this high-end spot in the Pearl District. *andinarestaurant.com; 5-9pm*

Pizza

Escape from NY Pizza $

 B4

The closest thing you'll find to New York–style pizza in Portland, served by the slice at this Nob Hill spot. *efnypizza.net; 11:30am-11pm*

Oven and Shaker $$

26 G5

Pizza and beer may go hand in hand, but so do pizza and craft cocktails. See for yourself at this pizzeria, which offers great cocktails and wood-fired pies with gourmet toppings (think Calabrese salami and pork belly). *ovenandshaker.com; 11:30am-9pm Sun-Thu, to 10pm Fri & Sat*

Drinking

Brewery

Breakside Brewery

 C2

This spacious Slabtown brewery is a pilgrimage destination for beer-lovers, as it's the only place you can get some of Breakside's coveted special brews on tap. *breakside.com/our_location/slabtown-pub-brewery; noon-9pm*

Deschutes Brewery Portland Public House

 G5

You don't have to go to Central Oregon to try craft beers made by this celebrated Bend brewery. The Portland outpost has over two dozen beers on tap, including specials that you won't find elsewhere. *deschutesbrewery.com/pages/portland-public-house; 11:30am-9pm Mon-Thu, to 10pm Fri & Sat*

Cocktails

Fools and Horses

 G5

This darkly lit bourgeois-bohemian hangout serves cocktails that are almost too pretty to drink, along with loosely French-inspired small plates and local oysters. *foolsandhorsespdx.com; 4-11pm Tue-Thu, to 1am Fri & Sat*

Palomar

 B2

This pretty-in-pink cocktail bar with a restaurant serves an extensive menu of tropical cocktails, many of which are blended to a frosty, frothy consistency. The food is great, too, featuring Cuban-inspired sandwiches and seafood plates. *barpalomar.com; 5-10pm*

The Pharmacy

 C5

Housed in a former pharmacy, this aptly named bar may not let you fill your prescriptions, but it will make you feel like you're in an old-timey apothecary-turned-speakeasy. *thepharmacypdx.com;*

2pm-2am Mon-Fri, noon-2am Sat & Sun*

Pope House Bourbon Lounge

 C5

Despite the name, you can get other tipples besides bourbon at this cocktail lounge, including a few zero-proof options. Still, the bourbon selection is vast and includes a selection of private barrel bourbons shipped in from Kentucky. *popehouselounge.com; 4pm-midnight Mon-Thu, to 1am Fri & Sat*

Teardrop Lounge

 G5

This sleek cocktail lounge in the Pearl District has been serving up elegant craft cocktails paired with flavorful small plates for nearly two decades. *teardroplounge.com; 4pm-12:30am Mon-Thu, to 2am Fri & Sat*

Mezcaleria

Comala

 H5

Move over tequila: mezcal is having a moment. Try it for yourself at this sweet spot specializing in the beloved Mexican spirit. *barcomala.com; 5-11pm Wed-Thu, to midnight Fri & Sat, to 10pm Sun*

Shopping

Chocolate

The Meadow

 B4

Artisanal chocolates by Oregon and international purveyors are reason enough to swing by this Nob Hill shop, which also has a great selection of cocktail bitters and finishing salts. *themeadow.com; 10am-8pm*

Verdun Chocolates

 G5

Treat yourself to hand-crafted, preservative-free chocolates and Jordan almonds from this oh-so-sweet Pearl District boutique. *verdunchocolates.com; 11am-6pm Mon-Sat, to 5pm Sun*

Gifts

MadeHere

 G6

Creations by nearly 200 makers are showcased at this keeping-it-local spot. Apparel, candles, cutting boards and chocolate treats are just a few of the many offerings. *madehereonline.com; 11am-6pm*

Hello from Portland

38 G6

Make a pit stop at this gift store for locally made, Portland- and Northwest-themed souvenirs, including T-shirts, snacks and body care. *hellofromportland.net; 10am-7pm*

Porch Light

 G5

Browse home goodies at this bright shop, which sells everything from candles and kitchenware to hard-to-find houseplants. *porchlightshop.com; 11am-5pm Sun-Tue, to 6pm Thu-Sat*

Stationery

Oblation Papers & Press

40 F5

Find handmade paper goods from around the world or pick up Oblation's own letter-pressed creations at this Pearl District institution. *oblationpapers.com; 11am-6pm Mon-Sat, noon-5pm Sun*

Paper Source

41 B4

Pick up pretty gifts, elegant wrapping paper and fun cards for every occasion. *papersource.com; 10am-7pm Mon, Tue & Sat, to 8pm Fri & Sat, 11am-6pm Sun*

See p98
for eating, drinking and shopping listings

Explore Northeast & North Portland

Researched by Margot Bigg

Artsy neighborhoods and great dining are what draw most people to the northeastern part of Portland, but for many decades this part of the city was largely residential. Starting in the late 1990s, many of the area's historically Black neighborhoods – notably the Albina area and the area around Alberta and Killingsworth Sts – began undergoing a process of gentrification, for better or worse. This is most evident on main drags such as the popular Alberta Arts District, an approximately 20-block stretch along NE Alberta St, and along North Mississippi, Vancouver and Williams Aves, where you'll find many of Portland's top restaurants.

Getting Around

MAX Light Rail

The Red, Blue, Green and Yellow Lines of the MAX stop at the Rose Quarter Transit Center. The Yellow Line continues north up to the Albina/Mississippi neighborhoods, while the Red Line continues northeast to the airport.

Streetcar

The Portland Streetcar's A and B Loops travel along Martin Luther King Jr Blvd and Grand Ave, respectively, looping through Northeast, Southeast, Northwest and downtown Portland.

Bus

Bus route 8 connects downtown to the Alberta Arts District (get off at NE 15th and Alberta).

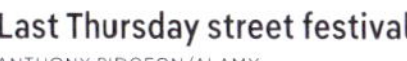

Last Thursday street festival
ANTHONY PIDGEON/ALAMY

THE BEST

HYDROTHERAPY SPA
Cascada Thermal Springs + Hotel (p96)

CITY SANCTUARY
The Grotto (p97)

SCHOOL FOR GROWNUPS
McMenamins Kennedy School (p92)

PLACE TO SMELL THE ROSES
Peninsula Park (p96)

STREET FAIR
Last Thursday on Alberta (p97)

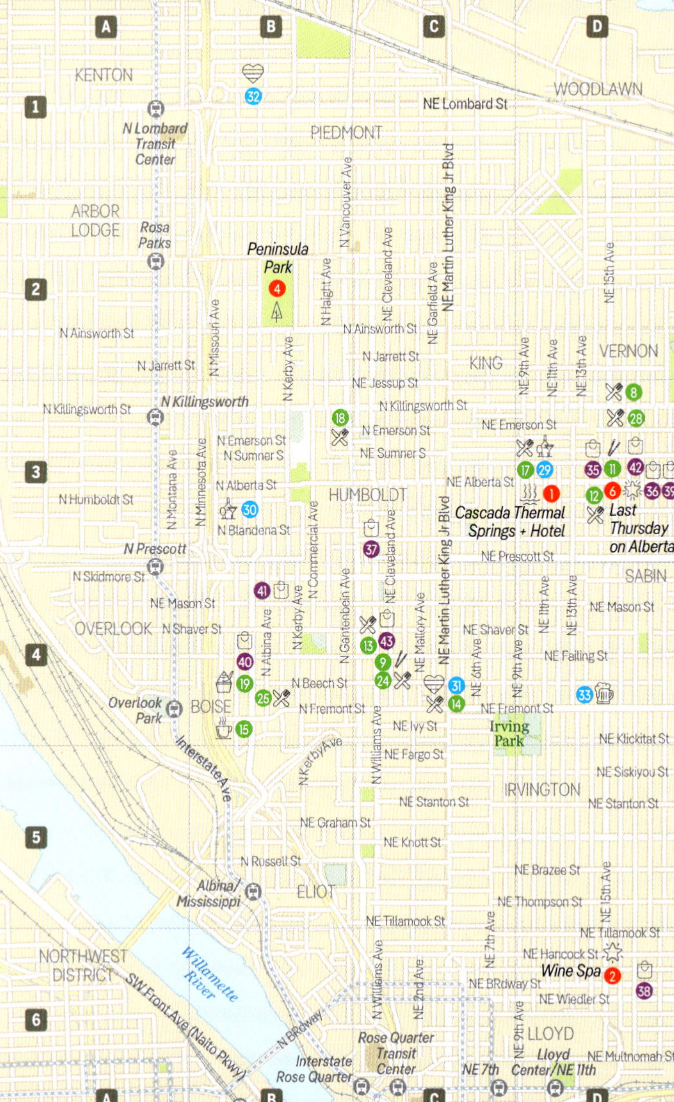
A
B
C
D
1
2
3
4
5
6
KENTON
WOODLAWN
NE Lombard St
PIEDMONT
N Lombard Transit Center
ARBOR LODGE
Rosa Parks
Peninsula Park
N Vancouver Ave
NE Cleveland Ave
NE Martin Luther King Jr Blvd
NE Garfield Ave
N Haight Ave
NE 15th Ave
N Ainsworth St
N Jarrett St
N Missouri Ave
N Kerby Ave
NE Jessup St
KING
NE 9th Ave
NE 11th Ave
NE 13th Ave
VERNON
N Killingsworth St
N Killingsworth
N Emerson St
NE Emerson St
N Sumner S
NE Sumner S
N Montana Ave
N Minnesota Ave
N Alberta St
NE Alberta St
N Humboldt St
HUMBOLDT
N Blandena St
N Commercial Ave
Cascada Thermal Springs + Hotel
Last Thursday on Alberta
N Prescott
NE Prescott St
N Skidmore St
SABIN
NE Mason St
N Gantenbein Ave
NE Mallory Ave
OVERLOOK
N Shaver St
NE Shaver St
NE Failing St
N Albina Ave
NE 6th Ave
N Beech St
Overlook Park
BOISE
N Fremont St
NE Fremont St
N Williams Ave
NE Ivy St
Irving Park
NE Klickitat St
Interstate Ave
N Kerby Ave
NE Fargo St
NE Siskiyou St
IRVINGTON
NE Stanton St
NE Graham St
NE Knott St
N Russell St
NE Brazee St
Albina/Mississippi
ELIOT
NE Thompson St
NE Tillamook St
NE 7th Ave
NORTHWEST DISTRICT
Willamette River
NE Hancock St
Wine Spa
NE 2nd Ave
NE BRdway St
SW Front Ave (Naito Pkwy)
NE Wiedler St
N BRdway
LLOYD
Rose Quarter Transit Center
Interstate Rose Quarter
NE 7th
Lloyd Center/NE 11th
NE Multnomah St
1
2
4
6
8
9
11
12
13
14
15
17
18
19
24
25
28
29
30
31
32
33
35
36
37
38
39
40
41
42
43

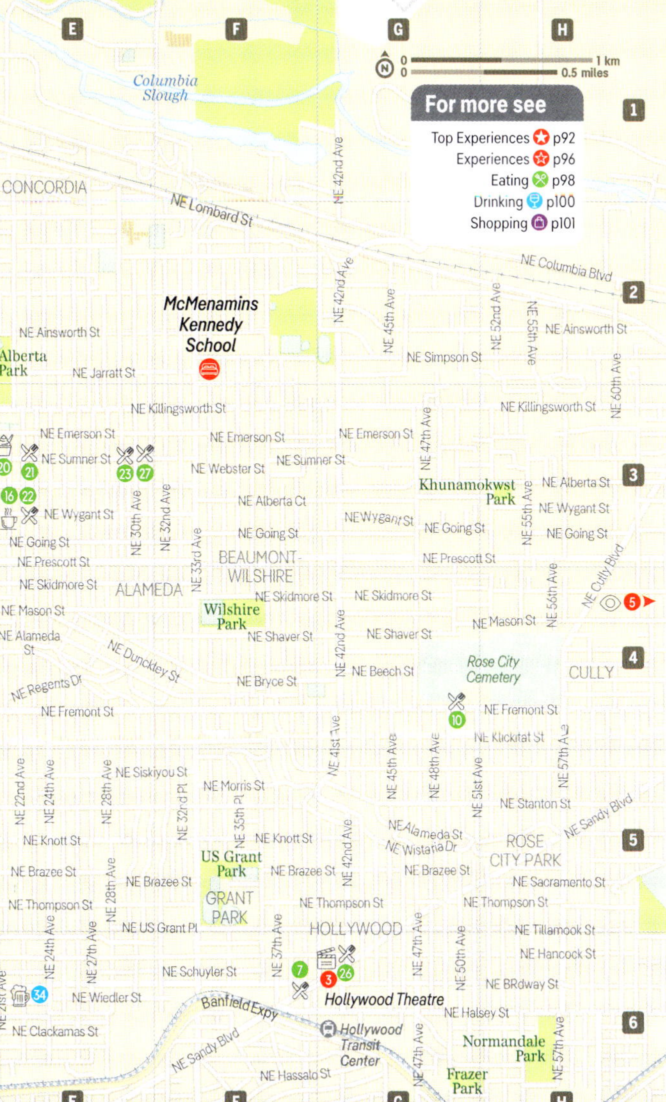

For more see
Top Experiences p92
Experiences p96
Eating p98
Drinking p100
Shopping p101
McMenamins Kennedy School
Hollywood Theatre
Hollywood Transit Center
Columbia Slough
CONCORDIA
ALAMEDA
BEAUMONT-WILSHIRE
CULLY
ROSE CITY PARK
GRANT PARK
HOLLYWOOD
Alberta Park
Wilshire Park
Khunamokwst Park
Rose City Cemetery
US Grant Park
Normandale Park
Frazer Park
NE Lombard St
NE Columbia Blvd
NE Sandy Blvd
NE Cully Blvd
Banfield Expy

★ TOP EXPERIENCE

McMenamins Kennedy School

Make your childhood dreams – or nightmares – of spending the night at school a reality at the Kennedy School, a 1915 elementary school that's been converted into a hospitality complex. Spend the night in a converted classroom or come for an evening dip in the outdoor soaking pool.

MAP P91 **F2**

PLANNING TIP
The Kennedy School Soaking Pool is popular, and free for neighborhood residents, so it can fill up. Book ahead to guarantee your soak.

Scan for information.

History Lessons

From 1915 until it closed in 1975, the John D Kennedy Elementary School was an active elementary school, and many of its original scholastic features remain to this day. The building was purchased in the mid-1990s by brothers Brian and Mike McMenamin. The duo transformed the school's old classrooms and administrative offices into guest rooms, pubs and bars, and soon the school was welcoming the community once again.

Back to Class

Overnight guests have the option of spending the night in converted classrooms with chalkboards and cloakrooms, or in the newer English Wing, which has 22 literature-inspired rooms. While staying the night is the best way to get the full Kennedy School experience, you don't need to be a hotel resident to enjoy the grounds of the old school.

Come on any given night and you'll find plenty of Portlanders rubbing shoulders with overnight guests, particularly at the massive **Boiler Room Bar**, a multistory pub that occupies the original boiler room (the original boiler is still on display). There are also a few smaller bars, including the

KAT NYBERG/ MCMENAMINS

reggae-themed Cypress Room rum bar and an indoor-outdoor Courtyard Restaurant. The **Kennedy School Theater** is another huge draw, with comfy sofa-style seating and tables so you can enjoy a beer and a slice of pizza while watching a movie.

The Soaking Pool

Among the Kennedy School's biggest draws is its heated outdoor soaking pool, a shallow warm-water pool designed for therapeutic dips. This steaming pool is tucked away in a private courtyard that's surrounded by greenery. Those who aren't hotel guests are welcome to soak between 10:30am and 7:30pm (reservations recommended), while those staying in the hotel can come early and stay late. Don't forget your swimsuit and towel!

QUICK BREAK

For a quick pick-me-up, head to the **Detention Bar**, which offers whiskey and cigars (for outdoor smoking) along with beer and snacks. Detention has never been so fun.

WALKING TOUR

Walk Northeast Portland

Northeast Portland's Alberta St is at its busiest during the monthly Last Thursday celebrations. It's a fun place to explore no matter when you make it to Portland. While you can do this walk in half an hour, it's best to slow down and make the most of the stops along the way.

START	END	LENGTH
Cascada Thermal Springs + Hotel	Alberta Rose Theatre	1 mile; 30 minutes

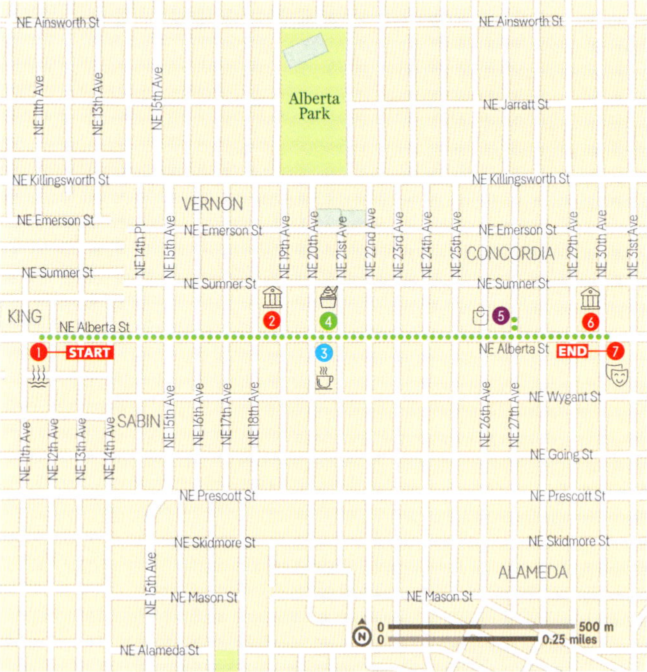

1 City Soak

Start your stroll down Alberta at **Cascada Thermal Springs + Hotel**, one of the newest spots on the street. Check out the biophilic design in the lobby, or book a massage or thermal session at the two-story spa, which includes a subterranean steam-and-soak circuit and a plant-filled atrium with a warm swimming pool.

2 Buy Local

After your soak, head to **Alberta Studios**, a collective of boutiques and artist studios. The vendors are always changing at this alternative shopping center, but expect to find a good selection of handmade items and vintage apparel no matter when you visit.

3 Flat White

Continue up the street to visit the first US outpost of Australian coffee company **Proud Mary** (p101). Grab a cup of coffee and continue your walk or stop for a hearty breakfast of avocado or eggs on toast.

4 The Latest Scoop

If you see a large group of people waiting in line, you've made it to **Salt & Straw** (p101), Portland's most popular homegrown ice-cream brand. Select your scoop from a menu of unusual flavors that change by the month, or play it safe by opting for one of the always-available bestsellers, such as chocolate brownie. Don't do dairy? Not to worry: there are always a few vegan options available.

5 Book Nook

Art buffs, bookworms and those who identify as both will want to give themselves extra time to browse the tomes and gifts at **Monograph Bookwerks**. Search for rare new and used books, pick up vintage-art opening posters and lettering charts or take home treasures that could range from vintage Keith Haring buttons to one-of-a-kind ceramic pieces.

6 Art on Alberta

Next, head to **Guardino Gallery**, which is among the oldest art institutions on Alberta St. This gallery has been showcasing works of local artists since it opened back in 1997, and is a great place to go if you want to understand why Alberta is known as one of Portland's main artistic neighborhoods.

7 Curtain Call

Wrap your walk up at **Alberta Rose Theatre**, a performing-arts venue that originally opened as a movie theater back in 1926. Originally called the Alameda Theatre, the Alberta Rose was a major hub for African American films in the 1970s, and was the place to see films such as *Abar: The First Black Superman* and *Mahogany*.

EXPERIENCES

Soak Away Your Troubles at Northeast Portland Spas

WELLNESS

Northeast Portland has transformed into a wellness destination in recent years. On Alberta St, **Cascada Thermal Springs + Hotel** (MAP: 1 P90 D3; *cascada.me*) draws in the wellness set with its massive spa, complete with a two-story thermal complex (which, despite being called a 'spring,' is fed with municipal water). On the street level is a massive conservatory with a 25ft wall of plants and big windows that let in lots of light. Below the conservatory is a subterranean hydrotherapy circuit with a steam room, a sauna and four soaking pools; an hour or two of soaking is enough for most people. Day passes are available to all who want to go for a soak; overnight guests get a half-off discount.

For a completely different approach to wellness – and to wine – book a treatment at the **Wine Spa** (MAP: 2 P90 D6; *thewinespapdx.com*). As the name suggests, this compact day spa focuses on wine, offering a range of 'vinotherapy' facials and treatments that make use of wine-sourced ingredients, such as resveratrol, to get your skin glowing. For an extra boost, add a pre-treatment wine bath to your experience.

Watch Indie Cinema at Hollywood Theatre

CINEMA

MAP: 3 P91 G6

Film fans flock to **Hollywood Theatre** *(hollywoodtheatre.org)*, not just for its solid lineup of independent movies and film fests, but also for its over-the-top facade. The Spanish Colonial–style frontage makes this former vaudeville theater look like it was conceived by Gaudí on mescaline, while the old 70mm projector used inside adds a vintage je ne sais quoi to the filmgoing experience. You'll find a scaled-down minitheater inspired by the Northeast Portland original in Concourse C of Portland International Airport. If you have a few minutes before your flight, it's worth stepping inside to watch a short film by a Pacific Northwest filmmaker.

Smell the Roses at Peninsula Park

PARK

MAP: 4 P90 B2

Portland is nicknamed the Rose City, and Peninsula Park is one of the places that shows how well-earned this nickname is. Site of the first public rose garden in town, this expansive park features a near-symmetrical arrangement of fragrant rose bushes and a large fountain. Other features include a massive field, an old-timey bandstand and a splash pad for little ones. The park was designed by

LAST THURSDAY

Alberta St (also known as the **Alberta Arts District**) is popular for its restaurants, bars, galleries and boutiques, but it's best experienced on the last Thursday evening of the month when special programming and gallery openings take place. In June, July and August, the stretch of Alberta between NE 15th and 30th Aves closes to traffic, and the area transforms into a giant street fair, aptly known as 'Last Thursday.' Expect street-side art vendors, DJs, food trucks and big crowds at this family-friendly affair. MAP: 6 P90 **D3**

Frederick Law Olmstead, who was one of the two landscape architects behind Central Park in Manhattan.

Find Solace at the Grotto

GARDEN

MAP: 5 P91 **H4**

One of the most tranquil places in Northeast Portland sits in an unlikely location: just past the intersection of two of the quadrant's busiest streets (NE 82nd Ave and NE Sandy Blvd). **The Grotto** (*thegrotto.org;* pictured), officially known as the National Sanctuary of our Sorrowful Mother, is a sprawling outdoor shrine dedicated to the Virgin Mary. Despite its Catholic affiliations, however, this forested Marian site is a hit among visitors of all faiths (or lack thereof) because of its pretty surroundings and its **upper-level garden** *(adult/child $9.95/4.95),* which is perched atop a basalt cliff. Though the Grotto is a year-round attraction, it draws the biggest crowds in the weeks leading up to Christmas, when it's adorned with upwards of two million holiday lights in honor of the annual Festival of Lights.

SEAN ATTILIO LEARN/SHUTTERSTOCK

LISTINGS

Best Places for...

See p90 for map of locations

$ Budget $$ Midrange $$$ Top End

Eating

Asian

Gado Gado $$$
7 F6
Head to this inventive, James Beard Award–nominated restaurant for Indonesian-inspired dishes and yummy cocktails. A special chili crab dinner takes place on Sundays and Mondays (with reservations). *gadogadopdx.com; 5-9pm*

Hat Yai $$
8 D3
Try casual Southern Thai bites and crisp fried chicken at this casual counter-style spot on Killingsworth. *hatyaipdx.com/killingsworth; 11:30am-3pm & 4-9pm Sun-Thu, to 10pm Fri & Sat*

Kayo's Ramen Bar $$
9 C4
Enjoy huge bowls of ramen on the covered patio of this popular spot on trendy N Williams Ave. There's plenty for vegan and gluten-free diners, too. *kayosramen.com; hours vary*

Nepali Kitchen and Chai Garden $
10 G4
Dine on Tibetan *momos* (dumplings) and other Himalayan treats at this cozy garden cafe with semi-enclosed seating nooks. *11am-7pm Thu-Mon*

Brunch

Mémoire Cà Phê $$
11 D3
American brunch classics meet Vietnamese flavors and cooking styles at this Alberta Arts District cafe. *memoire-ca-phe.square.site; 8am-2pm*

Tin Shed Garden Cafe $$
12 D3
Bring your dog to the outdoor patio of this long-time Alberta St brunch cafe. Many of the dishes have canine-inspired names. Try the Fetch, a bacon scramble served with grits or potato cakes. *tinshedgardencafe.com; 8am-2pm Mon-Fri, 7am-3pm Sat & Sun*

Caribbean

TapTap Cuisine $$
13 C4
Sample homestyle Haitian cuisine, including stews and fried plantains, at this family-run restaurant that caters to vegans and meat-lovers in equal measures. *taptapcuisine.com; 4-10pm Tue-Fri, noon-10pm Sat & Sun*

Yaad Style Jamaican Cuisine $$
14 C4
This Jamaican spot serves up big plates of jerk meat (or tofu) over rice and beans. *orderyaadstyle.com; 11am-8pm Tue-Sat, noon-7pm Sun*

Coffee

Cafe Rosetta $
15 B4
Delight in beautifully presented coffee drinks and sandwiches served on freshly baked focaccia at this new spot on Fremont St. *rosettapdx.com; 7:30am-3pm*

Proud Mary $

 E3

Embrace your inner Aussie by ordering a flat white with your avocado toast at the Alberta St branch of this popular coffee company from down under. *proudmarycoffee.com/ pages/portland-cafe; 8am-4pm*

Ethiopian

Bole Ethiopian Restaurant $

 D3

This popular spot features both vegetarian and meat-based dishes with a clearly marked menu so you know what's spicy and what's mild. *boleethio.com; noon-10pm Mon-Wed, Fri & Sat*

Enat Kitchen $$

 B3

This beloved restaurant offers massive platters available for one person, couples or whole families. Try the Ethiopian honey wine with your meal, or go the non-alcoholic route with honey water. *enat-kitchen.mxstorefront. com; noon-9pm Tue-Sat, 9am-9pm Thu*

Ice Cream

Kate's Ice Cream $

 B4

Choose from signature flavors such as orange creamsicle and ever-so Oregonian marionberry cobbler at this dairy- and gluten-free artisanal ice-cream spot, or opt for a seasonal treat. *katesice cream.com; 2-9pm Mon-Thu, Sat & Sun*

Salt & Straw $

 E3

A Portland institution for over a decade. Sweet-toothed locals stand in line for its flavorful scoops. *saltandstraw. com; 11am-11pm*

Mexican

Chilango $$

 E3

Mexico City street food is centered at this plant-based *taqueria* in the heart of the Alberta Arts District. *chilangopdx.com; noon-8pm Wed-Mon*

El Nutri Taco $

 E3

Order from a large menu of big, hearty burritos, taco salads, tacos, tortas and more at this no-frills neighborhood spot. *elnu-tritacopdx.com; 11am-7pm Mon-Sat*

Middle Eastern

DarSalam Restaurant $$

 E3

Try Middle Eastern dishes such as shish kabob, eggplant stew, mezze and more at this Iraqi spot. Don't miss the Iraqi pilsner, which is leveled up with rose water and cardamom. *darsalamres taurant.com; 4-9pm Mon-Thu, 11am-9pm Fri-Sun*

Mamma Khouri's $$

 C4

An extensive menu of Mediterranean dishes, from *mujadara* and stuffed grape leaves to shawarma and falafel sandwiches, make this Jordanian spot on N Williams an attractive option for hungry diners who want a bit of everything. *mamakhouris.com; 11am-9pm Mon-Sat*

Pizza

Mississippi Pizza $

 B4

Come for a slice and a pint and stay for live music and trivia nights at this popular neighborhood hangout on Mississippi Ave. *mississip pipizza.com; 11am-11pm, to midnight Fri & Sat*

Sizzle Pie $

 G6

Heavy metal blasts through speakers at the Sandy Blvd location of this Portland institution, where inventive pizzas get cheeky names (think Spiral Tap and Napalm Breath). The Rabbit's Salad is to die for. *siz zlepie.co; 11am-10pm*

Spanish

Urdaneta $$$

 E3

Gourmet Spanish cuisine paired with an extensive menu of vermouth makes this compact spot a great choice for a food-fueled date night. *urdanetapdx.com; 5-10pm Tue-Sun*

Vegan & Vegetarian

Feral $$

 D3

The menu is always evolving at this plant-powered restaurant, where chefs whip up inventive dishes from locally sourced and foraged ingredients for dinner. They occasionally open for special brunches, too. *feralvegan.com; 5-9pm Wed-Thu, to 10pm Fri & Sat*

Drinking

Cocktails

Bye and Bye

 D3

This spacious bar in the Alberta Arts District offers a huge covered patio that's great for outdoor drinking no matter the season. *theb yeandbye.com; hours vary*

Victoria Bar

 B3

Creative cocktails infused with flavors such as Earl Grey and coconut demerara sugar steal the show at this beloved cocktail bar. The Southern-inspired food menu is great, too. *victoriapdx.com; hours vary*

LGBTIQ+

Back2Earth

 C4

Regular DJ nights pack the dance floor at this welcoming spot, which attracts people of all genders and orientations. Video games and a massive plant wall add to the fun. *back2earthpdx.com; 7pm-1am Tue-Thu, to 2am Fri & Sat*

Eagle Portland

 B1

Owned by the same person as Back2Earth, the Eagle attracts a primarily gay male crowd with pool tables, leather contests and karaoke. *eagleport land.com; 2pm-2am*

Pub

Rose City Book Pub

 D4

Books and beer (and wine) pair together perfectly at this community pub with a great collection of used books that you can read while you sip or buy for later consumption. *rosecitybookpub.com; noon-midnight Mon-Fri, 11am-midnight Sat & Sun*

Rose & Thistle Public House

 E6

Pair British beer with pub classics such as Scotch eggs and fish and chips at this hole-in-the-wall pub in the Hollywood District. *roseandthistlepdx.com; 3pm-1am, Mon-Thu, 1pm-1am Fri-Sun*

Shopping

Apparel

Frock Boutique

 D3

Try on cute fits by designers from Portland and beyond at this friendly neighborhood boutique in the Alberta Arts District. *frockboutique.com; 10am-5pm*

Tumbleweed

 D3

European and US-made dresses, slacks and tops bring fashion-savvy shoppers with deepish pockets to this Alberta St boutique. Tumbleweed also has its own fashion line, kara-line. *tumble weedboutique.com; noon-5pm Mon-Fri, 11am-5pm Sat & Sun*

Books

Always Here Bookstore

37 C3

This worker-owned bookstore focuses on books with LGBTIQ+ themes and books by authors from the community. *alwaysherebooks.com; 11am-6pm Wed-Sun*

Broadway Books

 D6

This neighborhood bookstore is packed to the gills with fiction and non-fiction titles. It also offers regular readings and a curated book subscription box program. *broadwaybooks.net; 10am-6pm Tue-Fri, to 5pm Sat, 11am-5pm Sun*

Gifts & Decor

Ecovibe

 D3

This home-goods shop in the Alberta Arts District sells eco-friendly housewares and decor, plus a large selection of house plants. *ecovibestyle.com; 10am-6pm*

Gifty Kitty

 B4

Cat-lovers will find everything to tickle their feline fancy at this gift store, which features cat-themed gifts and housewares plus original kitty paintings by Portland artists. *giftykitty.com; 11am-7pm Mon-Thur, to 8pm Fri-Sun*

Paxton Gate

 B4

Take home your own selection of oddities from the Mississippi Ave location of this curiosity shop. Items on sale here are inspired by the natural world and include fossils, taxidermy and a wide selection of air plants. *paxtongate.com; 11am-7pm*

Wine

Cherries & Figs Wine Shop

 D3

Pick up wines from around the world at this intimate, BIPOC-owned wine shop in the heart of the Alberta Arts District. *cherriesandfigs.com; 11am-6pm Tue-Sat, to 5pm Sun & Mon*

Ora et Labora

 C4

Sit down for a wine flight or pick up a bottle to savor later at this neighborhood wine shop. Check the calendar for details on classes and workshops. *oraetlabora.wine; hours vary*

See p112
for eating,
drinking and
shopping
listings

Explore Southeast Portland

Researched by Margot Bigg

When people think of quintessential Portland, the city's Southeast quadrant often comes to mind. It's in this part of town where you'll find a mix of the city's classic arts-and-crafts homes – often fronted with lush gardens full of roses or planter boxes packed with dinosaur kale – as well as some of its best parks and family-friendly attractions. The Southeast is also home to loads of independent cafes, restaurants and shops, the bulk of which are concentrated on the trendy thoroughfares of Belmont St, Division St and Hawthorne Blvd, particularly in the 10 blocks west of César E Chavéz Blvd.

Getting Around

Bus

Southeast Portland is well served by bus. Major routes include the 14, which runs along Hawthorne St, and the 15, which travels up Belmont St, all the way up to the base of Mt Tabor Park.

Streetcar

The A and B Loops of the Portland Streetcar travel along Martin Luther King Jr Blvd and Grand Ave, respectively, and connect inner Southeast Portland with downtown Portland and parts of Northeast and Northwest.

MAX Light Rail

The MAX Orange Line connects downtown Portland with OMSI.

THE BEST

EDUCATIONAL ADVENTURE
OMSI (p162)

IMMERSIVE ART EXPERIENCE
Hopscotch Portland (p162)

PEACEFUL GARDEN
Crystal Springs Rhododendron Garden (p110)

QUIRKY MUSEUM
Portland Puppet Museum (p36)

CITY VIEWS
Mt Tabor Park (110)

Crystal Springs Rhododendron Garden (p110)
JPL DESIGNS/SHUTTERSTOCK

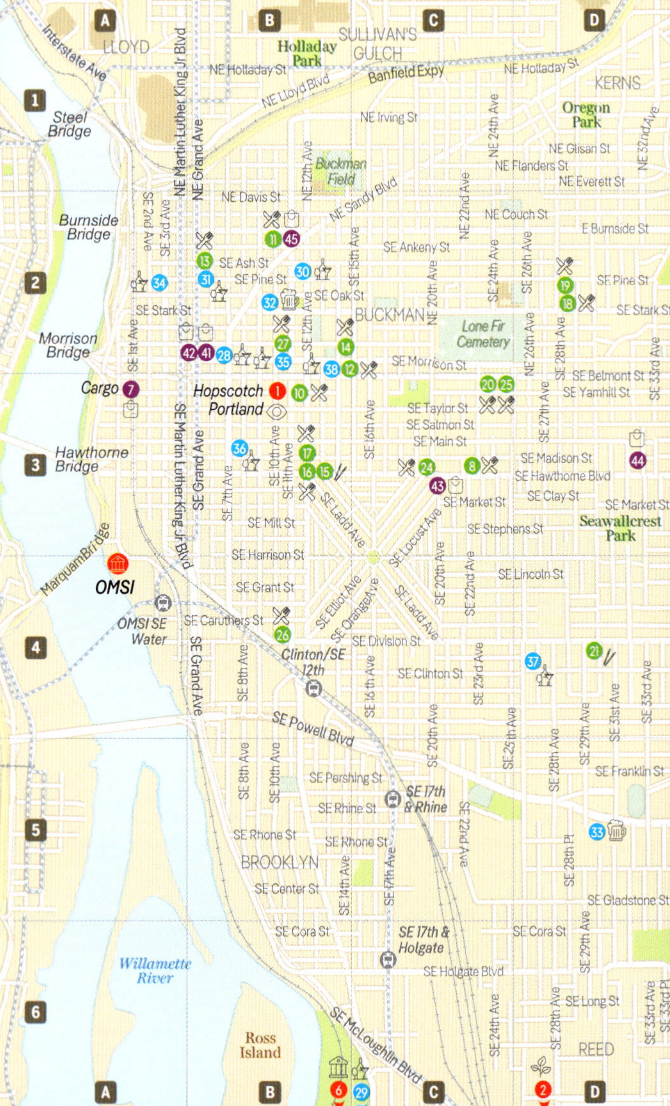
LLOYD
SULLIVAN'S GULCH
KERNS
BUCKMAN
BROOKLYN
REED
Holladay Park
Oregon Park
Buckman Field
Lone Fir Cemetery
Seawallcrest Park
Ross Island
Willamette River
Steel Bridge
Burnside Bridge
Morrison Bridge
Hawthorne Bridge
Marquam Bridge
Cargo
Hopscotch Portland
OMSI
OMSI SE Water
Clinton/SE 12th
SE 17th & Rhine
SE 17th & Holgate
Interstate Ave
NE Holladay St
NE Lloyd Blvd
Banfield Expy
NE Irving St
NE Sandy Blvd
NE Davis St
NE Glisan St
NE Flanders St
NE Everett St
NE Couch St
E Burnside St
SE Ankeny St
SE Ash St
SE Pine St
SE Oak St
SE Stark St
SE Morrison St
SE Belmont St
SE Yamhill St
SE Taylor St
SE Salmon St
SE Main St
SE Madison St
SE Hawthorne Blvd
SE Clay St
SE Market St
SE Mill St
SE Stephens St
SE Harrison St
SE Lincoln St
SE Grant St
SE Caruthers St
SE Division St
SE Clinton St
SE Powell Blvd
SE Franklin St
SE Pershing St
SE Rhine St
SE Rhone St
SE Center St
SE Gladstone St
SE Cora St
SE Holgate Blvd
SE Long St
SE McLoughlin Blvd
SE Ladd Ave
SE Locust Ave
SE Elliott Ave
SE Orange Ave
NE Martin Luther King Jr Blvd
NE Grand Ave
SE Martin Luther King Jr Blvd
SE Grand Ave
SE 1st Ave
SE 2nd Ave
SE 3rd Ave
SE 7th Ave
SE 8th Ave
SE 10th Ave
SE 11th Ave
NE 12th Ave
SE 12th Ave
SE 14th Ave
SE 15th Ave
SE 16th Ave
SE 17th Ave
NE 20th Ave
SE 20th Ave
NE 22nd Ave
SE 22nd Ave
SE 23rd Ave
NE 24th Ave
SE 24th Ave
SE 25th Ave
SE 26th Ave
NE 26th Ave
SE 27th Ave
SE 28th Ave
SE 28th Pl
SE 29th Ave
SE 31st Ave
NE 32nd Ave
SE 33rd Ave
SE 33rd Pl
A B C D
1 2 3 4 5 6

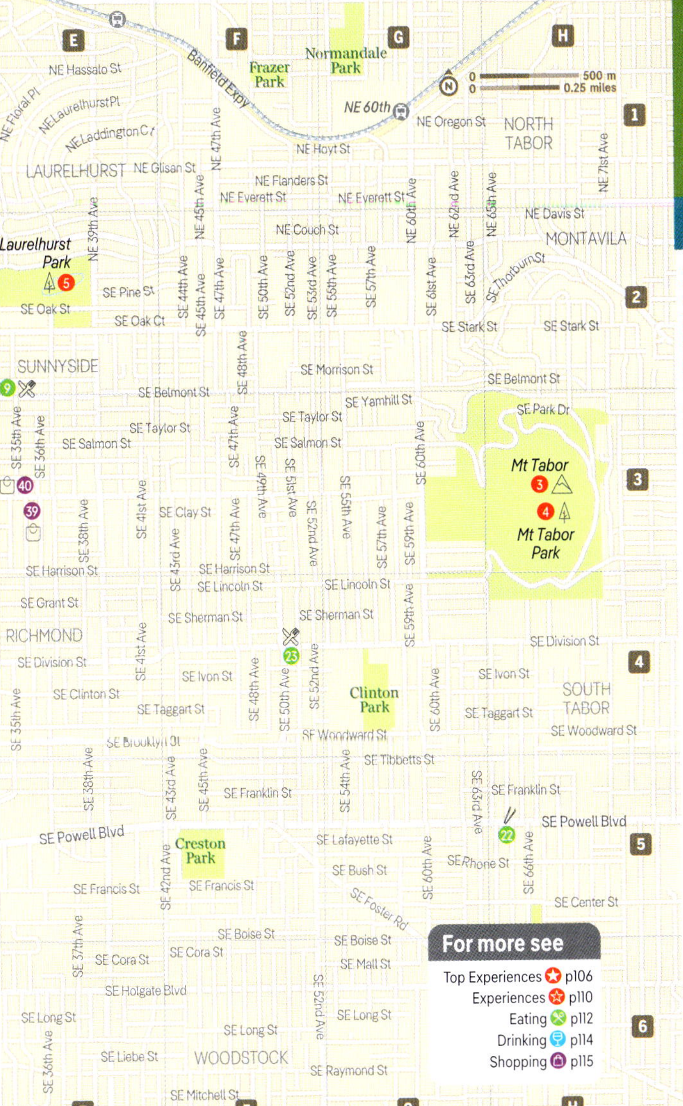

Laurelhurst Park
Normandale Park
Frazer Park
Mt Tabor
Mt Tabor Park
Clinton Park
Creston Park
LAURELHURST
NORTH TABOR
MONTAVILLA
SUNNYSIDE
RICHMOND
SOUTH TABOR
WOODSTOCK
Banfield Expy
NE 60th
500 m
0.25 miles
For more see
Top Experiences p106
Experiences p110
Eating p112
Drinking p114
Shopping p115

★ TOP EXPERIENCE

OMSI (Oregon Museum of Science & Industry)

Science and technology take center stage at OMSI, a spacious museum featuring a mix of hands-on exhibits and educational entertainment programming. While many of the exhibits are geared toward younger learners, OMSI offers an all-ages experience, and plenty of adults come here without kids.

MAP P104 **A4**

PLANNING TIP
Laser light shows, film screening and other special evening events often sell out in advance. It's best to book tickets online in advance if there's something you're dying to see.

Scan for information.

The OMSI Experience

Admission gets you access to the museum's permanent exhibits and labs, including the **Natural Sciences Hall**, with exhibits on topics ranging from rocks and minerals to prenatal development. **The Turbine Hall** is another big hit, thanks to its earthquake simulator, 'Epicenter,' which recreates the experience of being in quakes of varying magnitudes. The hall is also home to the **Curium**, a special space designed for children aged four to eight that features a massive wind instrument and a changing rotation of play labs. There's also a **Teen Tech Center** for over-13s, a science-themed playground for the under-six set and a **Space Science Hall**, complete with a planetarium.

The USS Blueback

One of OMSI's most popular features is the USS *Blueback*, a submarine docked in the Willamette River, right next to the main museum building. The Blueback was the last United States Navy diesel-electric sub to be used in active duty, and was once home to a resident crew of 85 submariners. Small-group tours capped at 12 people take guests into the 219ft sub multiple times throughout the

CARSON MATHIUS/SHUTTERSTOCK

day. If you're really into submarines, you can also sign up for a special three-hour tech-focused tour (held on the second and fourth Sunday of the month). These tours, led by submarine veterans, go into great detail about the inner workings of the Blueback, and submarines in general.

OMSI after Dark

While OMSI draws plenty of kids during daylight hours, come in the evening and you'll find a different scene. The museum's most popular evening activity is OMSI After Dark, a series of themed sessions on topics ranging from neuroscience to natural wonders. These shindigs, which typically take place on the last Wednesday of the month, are restricted to guests 21 and over and feature DJs, science demonstrations and drinking.

QUICK BREAK
Stop for a cup of coffee or a grab-and-go sandwich at the **Empirical Café**, located inside OMSI, next to its theater. Beer and wine are also available in the evening.

WALKING TOUR

Walk Southeast Portland

A great way to get a feel for Southeast Portland's vibe is by strolling along the shop- and restaurant-lined Hawthorne and Belmont Sts before making your way to Laurelhurst Park, a popular spot for strolling, picnicking and soaking in the sun during Portland's brief burst of summer sunshine.

START	END	LENGTH
Powell's Books	Laurelhurst Park	1.2 miles; 30 minutes

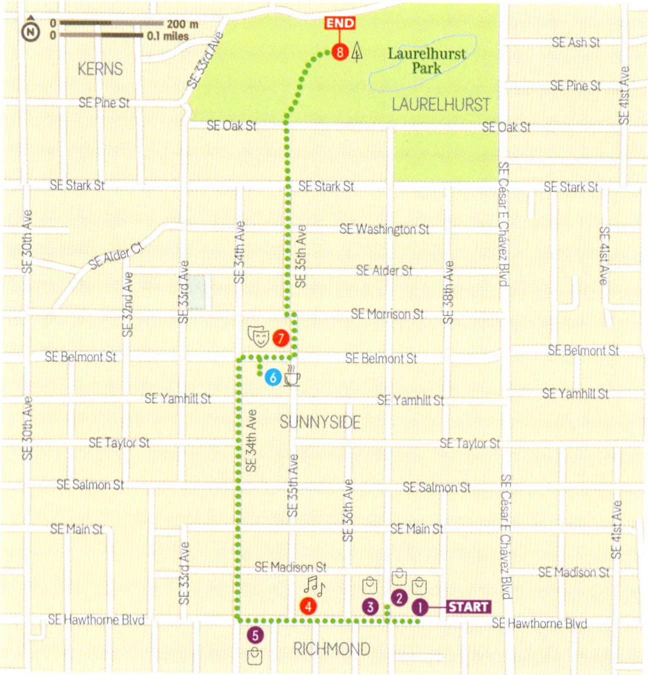

1 Eastside Bookworm

Start your walk at **Powell's Books on Hawthorne**, the eastside outpost of Portland's most famous bookstore. It's much smaller than the flagship Powell's City of Books in downtown, but still offers a huge array of new and used titles plus plenty of funky gift and souvenir items.

2 Gifts from Afar

Around the corner from Powell's, **Gold Door Jewelry & Arts** offers an eclectic, expertly curated collection of jewelry and decorative trinkets from around the world, from moonstone cabochons to statues of the Brazilian sea goddess Yemanjá.

3 Cards for All Occasions

Continue west down Hawthorne for a block until you reach **Presents of Mind**, a card and gift shop that's been delighting Portlanders with its vast selection of greeting cards and quirky gift items for generations. Parents take note: this little shop has one of the best selections of stickers (sold by the roll) in town.

4 Local Legends

If you're looking for uniquely Portland (and Oregon) gifts, head south one block to the Hawthorne St branch of **Tender Loving Empire**. This local record label and gift store hawks a mix of indie CDs, housewares, toiletries and snack items that are sourced almost entirely from local makers and artists.

5 Conscious Consumption

One more block west leads you to **Way of Being**, a 'low waste' concept store that sells an impressive selection of eco-friendly items (think biodegradable dishwasher tablets and bamboo everything).

6 Tea Time

From here, head along SE 34th Ave, past centuries-old arts-and-crafts homes and little free libraries until you reach Belmont St, home to the **Tao of Tea**, a beautiful tea room serving brews and small plates from around the world.

7 Playtime & Showtime

Across the street, the **Avalon Theatre** is a great place to watch movies for cheap, though many people come here for the theater's Wunderland Arcade, which draws in guests of all ages with its arcade games and pinball machines.

8 A Walk in the Park

Continue north for a few blocks and you'll reach **Laurelhurst Park**, a sprawling green space with a dog park, a duck pond and blocks of undulating green spaces flanked by paved jogging paths. Come in the summer and you may encounter headphone-clad dancers grooving to a silent disco.

EXPERIENCES

Immerse Yourself in Art at Hopscotch Portland
ART

MAP: 1 P104 **B3**

Jump into a ball pit full of color-changing bubbles, tag your name on a brick wall using lasers, or try to find your way out of a seemingly infinite hall of mirrors at **Hopscotch Portland** *(letshopscotch.com/locations/portland; adult/child $24/15)*. It's worth giving yourself a couple of hours to explore this interactive art space, which features 14 wonderfully whimsical immersive experiences created by artists from around the world. There's also a lounge slinging cocktails and snacks for a bit of post-play refueling.

Connect with Nature at Crystal Springs Rhododendron Garden
GARDEN

MAP: 2 P104 **D6**

Portland has plenty of beautiful gardens, but few are as pretty in the springtime as **Crystal Springs Rhododendron Garden** *(crystalspringsgardenpdx.org; adult/child $9/6)*. Tucked away between a golf course and a liberal-arts college, this 9.5-acre natural area features a gargantuan central pond that draws plenty of wildlife, including waterfowl and nutria (Oregon's less-popular cousin to the capybara). It's the rhododendron blooms that make this spot so special, but even if you visit outside their blooming season, it's still fun to wander the garden's meandering gravel paths.

Hang Out in Southeast Portland's Parks
PARK

Here's a fun Portland fact: the City of Roses is one of only a handful of US cities with its own extinct volcano, **Mt Tabor** (MAP: 3 P105 **H3**). Spread out over 191 acres over the top of that very volcano, **Mt Tabor Park** (MAP: 4 P105 **H3**) is one of the best spots in Portland to take in city views, especially if you come around sunset and face west toward downtown. It's also a great place for an invigorating uphill hike, offering an extensive trail system connecting the base of the park to the summit plus a long stretch of staircases if you want to take a direct, but literally breathtaking, way up.

For a lower-elevation place to wander, visit **Laurelhurst Park** (MAP: 5 P105 **E2**), a beautifully landscaped 30-acre park with surrounding a spring-fed pond that was a popular watering hole for cattle back in Portland's early years (these days it's a duck pond). Park highlights include paved walking paths, large grassy expanses that draw in serious picnicking crowds as soon as the sun begins to shine, and a playground.

See Marionettes & More at the Portland Puppet Museum

MUSEUM

MAP: 6 P104 **B6**

On a residential side street in Portland's Sellwood neighborhood, the **Portland Puppet Museum** *(puppetmuseum.com; by donation)* is one of the only puppetry-themed museums in the country. Step inside this one-room space to see a selection of puppets from around the world, from Balinese and Cambodian shadow puppets illuminated by light boxes to the former stars of Portland's erstwhile Tears of Joy Theatre. The museum preserves the massive collection of puppeteer-owner Steven Overton and his late partner Marty Richmond (the duo's puppet-led spin on 'The Tortoise and the Hare' is said to have inspired Stephen Sondheim's Broadway hit *Into the Woods*). The museum also hosts an array of special events, from puppet-making workshops to outdoor summer soirées and plays. Note that while the one-room museum is typically open Thursday to Sunday, 2pm to 8pm, hours can vary, so it's best to call ahead to make sure that someone's around to welcome you.

Find Treasures from Near & Far at Cargo

SHOPPING

MAP: 7 P104 **A3**

Occupying an old warehouse just a few blocks east of the Willamette River, **Cargo** *(cargoinc.com)* toes the line between a shop and a full-on experience. This massive showroom houses a number of small businesses that specialize in everything from scented skincare to vintage records. Ground-floor highlights include the **Venderia**, a vending machine stocked with everything from colored-lens glasses to mystery goody bags, and the **Rx Letterpress**, where artist Emily Riley cranks out cheeky (and, oftentimes, cat-themed) greeting cards using antique letterpresses. The lower level is full of decorative finds from around the world, which run the gamut from massive salvaged doors from India and Indonesia to vintage Japanese *kokeshi* dolls.

PDX ADULT SOAPBOX DERBY

If you're in Portland in August, don't miss the **Portland Adult Soapbox Derby** *(soapboxracer.org)*, held on the steep slopes of Mt Tabor Park. For over a quarter century, this annual event has allowed Portland soapbox-car engineers to show off their functional – and oftentimes fantastical – creations through a fast-paced, but friendly, race to the bottom.

LISTINGS

Best Places for...

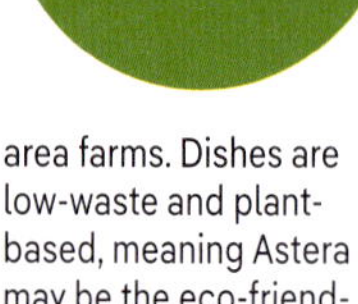
See p104 for map of locations

$ Budget $$ Midrange $$$ Top End

Eating

Breakfast & Brunch

Jam on Hawthorne $$

 8 C3

It's always breakfast time at this Portland classic known for innovative scrambles, hashes and Benedicts, plus great bloody Marys. *jamonhawthorne.com; 8am-2pm Mon-Fri, to 3pm Sat & Sun*

Paradox Cafe $

9 E2

An Old Portland classic, Paradox serves up hearty plates of mostly (but not exclusively) vegetarian breakfast and lunch dishes in a no-frills space with an aesthetic that's equal parts 1950s diner and Portland punk DIY. *paradoxorganiccafe.com; 9am-2:30pm Thu-Mon*

European

Kachka $$$

 10 B3

Kachka puts a Pacific Northwest spin on dishes from the region formerly known as the USSR. Fittingly, this local favorite also has a huge selection of vodka available. *kachkapdx.com; hours vary*

Normandie $$$

 11 B2

Pacific Coast dining meets French fare at Normandie. While the menu changes with the seasons, you're likely to find oysters, clams, cheese and charcuterie on the menu during your visit. *normandiepdx.com; 5-9pm Sun-Thu, to 10pm Fri & Sat*

Fine Dining

Astera $$$

12 B2

Beloved Portland chef Aaron Adams flexes his culinary prowess at his latest project, Astera, which offers beautifully plated tasting menus that showcase the bounty of area farms. Dishes are low-waste and plant-based, meaning Astera may be the eco-friendliest option in Portland. *asterapdx.com; hours vary Thu-Sun*

Kann $$$

 13 B2

Currently Portland's *it* restaurant, Kann specializes in Haitian wood-fired fare. It's owned by Gregory Gourdet, a James Beard Award–winning celebrity chef (you may have seen him on reality TV show, *Top Chef*). *kannrestaurant.com; 4-10pm Tue-Thu, to 11pm Fri & Sat*

Nostrana $$$

 14 B2

Italian fare meets Pacific Northwest ingredients at Nostrana, a classic dinner spot known for traditional meat and pasta dishes along with mighty fine pizza. The wine list is fantastic, too; don't miss the restaurant's own Barbera Nostrana. *nostrana.com; 5-9pm Mon-Thu, to 10pm Fri & Sat*

Food Carts

BKK Pad Thai $

 B3

Head to BKK Pad Thai in the Cartopia pod to get your fill of fried rice, yellow curry and, of course, pad Thai. *bkkpadthai.com; 11:30am-9:30pm Tue-Sun*

Potato Champion $

 B3

It's hard not to love potatoes, especially at Potato Champion, a long-established Portland food cart serving Belgian-style French fries with a variety of toppings, plus some pretty mean poutine. *potatochampion.com; 11am-10pm Tue-Thu, to 11pm Fri & Sat*

Tahrir Square $

 B3

Eat like an Egyptian at this beloved food cart. The menu features everything from falafel and dolmas to gyros and warming lentil soup. *instagram .com/tahrirsquarepdx; 11am-11pm*

Pizza

Baby Doll Pizza $

 D2

Don't miss the garlic knots at this no-frills pizzeria that draws in a late-night crowd. *baby dollpizza.com; 11am-11pm Sun-Thu to midnight Fri & Sat*

Ken's Artisan Pizza $$

 D2

Wood-fired pizza made with slow-fermented dough and primo ingredients makes the pies at this institution seem as sophisticated as they are tasty. *kensartisan.com/ pizza; 5-9pm Tue-Sat, to 10pm Fri & Sat, 4:30-9pm Sun*

Southeast Asian

Jade Rabbit $$

 C3

This cozy spot serves up a pan-Asian menu of delicious treats, with great dim sum (including adorable, bunny-shaped buns) and Filipino classics such as adobo. The tea service and cocktail and mocktail menu are top-notch, too. *jaderabbitpdx.com; hours vary Wed-Sun*

Kati Portland $$

 D4

Choose from classic noodle dishes and curries or opt for innovative treats such as *nam khao tod* (crisp rice served with a half-head of lettuce) at this neighborhood Thai spot. *katiportland.com; hours vary Thu-Tue*

Rose VL Deli $

 H5

While Rose VL Deli doesn't look like much from the outside (it's a simple spot in an unassuming strip mall), locals in the know will tell you that it's one of the best places for Vietnamese soup and *bánh mì* in town. *8:30am-4pm Mon, Tue & Thu-Sat*

Vegan & Vegetarian

DC Vegetarian $

23 F4

Chow down on filling submarine sandwiches and burgers without the meat at this low-key neighborhood spot. *dcvegetarian. com; 11am-8pm Tue-Sat, to 3pm Sun*

Maruti Indian Restaurant $$

24 C3

Indulge in hearty Indian dishes such as biryani and samosa *chole* at this Indian vegetarian spot, which also offers plenty for vegan and gluten-free diners. *maruti-restau rant.com; 4:30-8:30pm Wed-Mon*

Mirisata $$

 C3

Try spicy Sri Lankan curries and stuffed rotis at this worker-owned spot with a sprawling covered patio. Bonus points: workers receive above minimum wage and don't take tips. *mirisata.com; hours vary*

West African

Akadi $$

 B4

Go on a culinary journey through West Africa at Akadi, which serves savory stews served with jollof rice, pounded yam and the restaurant's own line of tasty carrot-based dipping sauces (you can buy them by the bottle, too). *akadipdx.com; 4-9pm Wed-Sun*

Kabba's Kitchen $$

 B2

Senegambian food is the star of the menu at the Southeast Portland location of this family-owned spot. Don't miss the pillowy plantains or the spicy chicken or fish yassa. *kabbaskitchenor.com; 11am-8pm Tue-Sat*

Drinking

Bars

Creepy's

 B2

As the name (sort of) suggests, this clown-themed bar is sure to give you the heebie-jeebies, or at least a good laugh. *creepyspdx.com; 4pm-1am Sun-Thu, to 2:30am Fri & Sat*

Bible Club

 C6

While you may not have a religious experience at this antique-adorned, speakeasy-style spot, you're sure to have a good cocktail. The heated, dog-friendly covered patio is an added bonus. *bibleclubpdx.com; 4pm-midnight Mon-Sat, to 11pm Sun*

Hungry Tiger

 B2

Vintage tiger images and a playlist that goes heavy on the punk rock add to the Old Portland appeal of this hip spin on a neighborhood dive bar. Pinball, pool, proper cocktails and vegan corn dogs add to the appeal. *hungrytigerpdx.com; hours vary*

Sousòl

 B2

Haitian Creole for 'basement,' this subterranean cocktail lounge serves tasty mocktails and cocktails paired with Caribbean-inspired snacks. It's a great place to try celebrity chef Gregory Gourdet's cuisine if you can't snag a reservation at Kann upstairs. *sousolbar.com; 4-11pm Thu-Sat*

Breweries

Bauman's on Oak

 B2

This laid back, all-ages cider room by Bauman's Century Farm has a range of tasty tipples, from tayberry-infused ciders to co-fermented cider and rosé. *baumanscider.com/baumansonoak; 4-9pm Wed & Thu, 2-9pm Fri & Sat*

Hopworks Urban Brewery

 D5

Try a sampler of five small cups of craft beer or commit to a full pint of pale ale, IPA or pilsner at this popular brew pub. *hopworksbeer.com; 11:30am-9pm Sun-Wed, to 10pm Thu-Sat*

Dance Floors

45 East

 A2

Big-name electronic acts pull in crowds at this club in the industrial eastside. The lasers on the dance floor can get intense. *45eastpdx.com; hours vary Thu-Sat*

Holocene

 B2

Housed in an old auto-parts warehouse, this popular venue has been hosting live acts and DJs for over two decades.

It has some of the best sound in town, thanks to a high-fidelity Danley sound system. *holocene.org; hours vary*

White Owl Social Club

This indoor/outdoor bar and restaurant holds plenty of dance parties, from nighttime house-music soirees to Sunday daytime events that draw in an early-to-bed crowd. *whiteowlsocialclub.com; hours vary Tue-Sun*

Wine Bars

Daydream

Sip on wine, vermouth, sake and mocktails from around the world at this compact neighborhood spot. Guest DJs spin everything from dub to downtempo on most Saturday nights. *favorite-neighbors.com; hours vary Wed-Sun*

Nectaris

Fine wine from Oregon and beyond meets European-inspired plant-based snacking (including dairy-free fondue) at this cozy spot in the Buckman neighborhood. *nectaris.wine; hours vary Thu-Sun*

Shopping

Apparel

Communion

Chic frocks and tailored trousers are just a sampling of what you'll find at this slightly expensive spot. *communionpdx.com; noon-6pm Wed-Fri, from 11am Sat & Sun*

Twill Boutique

This little boutique specializing in women's fashion and accessories showcases the works of smaller designers and brands that you won't easily find in other shops around town. *twillclothing.com; hours vary*

Books

Literary Arts Bookstore

This spacious bookstore, run by the city's main literary organization, features an expertly curated selection of books by authors from Portland and around the world. *bookstore.literary-arts.org; 9am-9pm Mon-Fri, 10am-9pm Sat & Sun*

Mother Foucault's Bookshop

Move over Powell's: this beloved bookstore offers an impressive selection of used and rare books, plus regular readings and lit events. *motherfoucaultsbookshop.com; noon-6pm*

Vintage

Magpie

This curated secondhand-apparel shop has been hawking timeless clothes since before vintage was mainstream. *instagram.com/magpievintage; noon-7pm Wed-Mon, 2-6pm Sun*

Telephone Vintage

Score everything from vintage jackets to antiques and electronics at this eclectic vintage emporium. *instagram.com/telephonevintage; 11am-7pm*

Yellowstone Vintage

45 B2

Browse through an expertly curated collection of secondhand clothing, accessories and furniture at this popular vintage spot. *instagram.com/yellowstonevtg; noon-5pm Thu-Mon*

★ WORTH A TRIP

The Columbia River Gorge

Stretching along the Columbia River, from just east of Portland to the Cascade Mountains, the Columbia River Gorge is among the most beautiful areas in the Pacific Northwest. This scenic stretch is known for great hiking trails, soaring cliffs that double as great viewpoints and loads of misty waterfalls.

GETTING THERE
The most flexible way to experience the gorge is by driving, but there are plenty of alternatives for non-drivers, including the Columbia Gorge Express bus, which travels from Portland to Hood River.

Scan for suggestions on what to see and do.

Vista House

Built in 1917 as a rest stop, the octagon-shaped **Vista House** *(vistahouse.com; free)* is worth visiting for its unusual architecture and its great views. It stands atop Crown Point, a 693ft promontory that looks out over the Columbia River, and is one of the first attractions you'll reach after heading east into the gorge from Portland. While many people stop here just to take in the views, it's worth heading inside the building, which features beautiful stained-glass windows and houses a small museum with interpretive displays in its marble-clad interiors. Head up to the roof for the best views around or descend into the basement where you'll find a couple of gift shops, a coffee shop and restrooms. Note that the house is open Friday to Monday, but you can visit the exterior and hang out in the parking lot whenever you want. The viewpoint is a popular destination for stargazers during special astral events such as the annual Perseids meteor shower and on the rare occasions when the northern lights are visible in northern Oregon.

Multnomah Falls & the Waterfall Corridor

Stretching for nearly 9 miles along the Historic Columbia River Hwy (Hwy 30), which runs

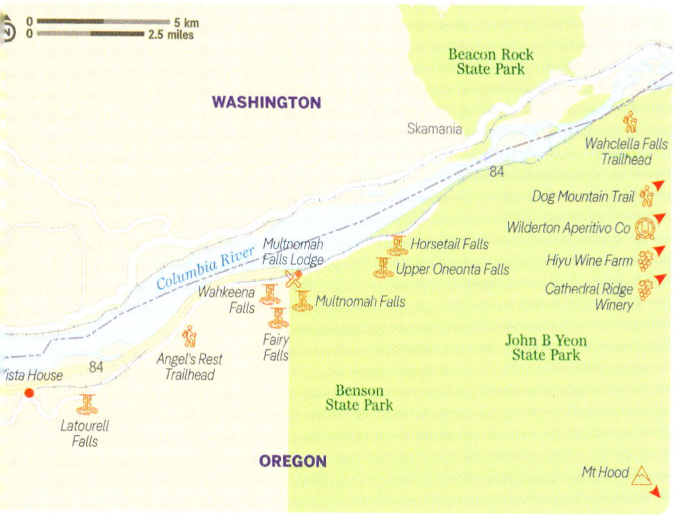

0 5 km
0 2.5 miles
Beacon Rock State Park
WASHINGTON
Skamania
Wahclella Falls Trailhead
84
Dog Mountain Trail
Wilderton Aperitivo Co
Multnomah Falls Lodge
Horsetail Falls
Hiyu Wine Farm
Columbia River
Upper Oneonta Falls
Cathedral Ridge Winery
Wahkeena Falls
Multnomah Falls
Fairy Falls
John B Yeon State Park
Angel's Rest Trailhead
'ista House
84
Benson State Park
Latourell Falls
OREGON
Mt Hood

parallel to I-84, the Waterfall Corridor very much lives up to its name, with a variety of beautiful waterfalls of all sorts. Some – such as the misty cascades of **Fairy Falls** – require a hike through the forest to get to; others, such as **Latourell Falls**, don't require much hiking at all.

To get to this scenic stretch by car, take I-85 to Corbett (exit 22) and continue north past the Vista House toward Latourell Falls. Continue onwards to **Wahkeena Falls**, where you can hike to Fairy Falls or continue to **Multnomah Falls**, the granddaddy of all Columbia Gorge waterfalls. This 620ft cascade is the tallest waterfall in Oregon, and while many people stop by just to take in views from the parking lot – and, perhaps, stop by the **Multnomah Falls Lodge** *(multnomahfallslodge.com)* for a snack and some souvenir shopping – it's well worth making the short walk

QUICK BREAK
For a refreshing spritzer that won't impair your ability to drive home afterward, stop by the **Wilderton Aperitivo Co** tasting room in Hood River for a non-alcoholic cocktail.

PLANNING TIP
Timed-use permits are required to visit Multnomah Falls between Memorial Day and Labor Day. For more information and to get a permit, visit *recreation.gov*.

up to Benson Bridge, which doubles as a viewing point over the falls, or hike a full 1.2 miles to the very top of the waterfall. After you've reached the top, you can hike back toward Wahkeena Falls via trail #420 or return to the bottom and continue your drive east, passing by the trailheads to **Upper Oneonta Falls** and **Horsetail Falls** along the way.

Columbia Gorge Hikes

Hiking opportunities in the Columbia Gorge abound, from short jaunts to waterfalls to more challenging hikes that can test the limits of regular hikers. For an easier hike that's good for novice hikers and families, consider the **Wahclella Falls Trail**, a 2.4-mile out-and-back stroll

HELMINADIA/SHUTTERSTOCK

through a slot canyon in the Mark O Hatfield Wilderness, west of the Waterfall Corridor. The hike leads to **Wahclella Falls** (pictured), a two-tiered fall that splashes into a large pool surrounded by moss-covered stones. For a more challenging alternative, head to the **Angel's Rest Trailhead** near Corbett. This popular 4.5-mile hike takes around three hours to complete and rewards hikers with incredible Columbia Gorge views – and, if you come in the late winter and spring, colorful wildflowers. If you really want to get your blood pumping, head to the Washington side of the Columbia River and take the trail up to the 2948ft summit of **Dog Mountain**. This 6.9-mile loop comes with a 2820ft elevation gain, and it's far from easy, especially on windy days, but the views are magnificent.

Hood River

At the eastern end of the Gorge, Hood River is a charming old city with epic views of Mt Hood and plenty of wineries and farm stands worth visiting. The city is considered the world's windsurfing capital, and while it's fun to watch windsurfers out on the Columbia, there's plenty more to do in the area. The region has a long tradition of pear and apple growing, with loads of U-pick spots and farm stands worth visiting. The best way to experience this aspect of the area is by driving the 35-mile **Hood River Fruit Loop** *(hoodriverfruitloop.com)*, which passes along bucolic back roads and past historic orchards, with lots of opportunities to stop and sample wine, cider and locally grown fruit.

MT HOOD

Many people pair a visit to the gorge with a trip to nearby Mt Hood, which offers a long skiing season and great summer hiking opportunities (plus an alpine slide).

HOOD RIVER WINERIES

The Columbia River Gorge area is a popular destination for wine tasting. Popular wineries include **Cathedral Ridge Winery** and **Hiyu Wine Farm**, both in Hood River.

★ WORTH A TRIP

The Oregon Coast

With 363 miles of sandy beaches and rocky headlands flanked by windswept trees and old-growth forests, the Oregon Coast is easily one of the state's most picturesque regions. It's also easy to get to from Portland, whether on a short day trip or a weekend getaway.

MAP **P125**

GETTING THERE
The quickest way to get to the coast from Portland is to take Hwy 26 (aka the Sunset Hwy) west to Hwy 101, the Oregon Coast Hwy.

Scan for practical information.

Astoria

The northernmost (and largest) city on the Oregon Coast, Astoria is also the oldest city in the state, with plenty of gorgeous 19th-century homes to show for it. One home in particular, the **Goonies House**, is particularly famous as it was used as Mikey's house in the 1985 cult classic, *The Goonies* (just be aware that the home is a residence and can only be viewed from outside). Film buffs can learn more about movies shot in Astoria (including *Free Willy* and *Kindergarten Cop*) at the **Oregon Film Museum**.

If history is more your jam, don't miss the Lewis and Clark National Historical Park, which preserves **Fort Clatsop**. It was here that the Lewis and Clark Expedition spent the final winter of their westward journey, from December 1805 until March 1806, and there's a great visitor center – and a reproduction of the fort – where you can learn more about the journey that set the stage for westward expansion. **Fort Stevens State Park** is another must-visit for history fans, especially those interested in military history. The fort was used until WWII and many of its old batteries are still intact. Visit Columbia Beach in the park to see the skeletal remains of the *Peter Iredale* (pictured), which shipwrecked in 1906.

HRACH HOVHANNISYAN/SHUTTERSTOCK

Cannon Beach

Cannon Beach is one of the two closest beach towns from Portland (the other is Seaside), and getting there from Portland usually takes around 90 minutes without traffic. This little town has some of the prettiest stretches of coastline on the North Coast, and its **Haystack Rock**, a 17-million-year-old sea stack, is one of the most photographed geological features in the state (bring binoculars and you may catch a glimpse of tufted puffins roosting on the rock). While the beach is a big draw, the town itself is also worth a visit for the cute boutiques and art galleries along its main thoroughfare, **Hemlock Street**.

On your way into (or out of) Cannon Beach, take a detour to **Ecola State Park** on the north side of town to take in the bluff-top views at **Ecola Point**. If you have a couple of hours to

QUICK BREAK

For a filling meal or to check out a particularly folksy gift shop, stop at **Camp 18** on Hwy 26, just a few miles east of the junction of Hwy 26 and the Oregon Coast Hwy.

spare, take the 2.1-mile trail down to nearby **Indian Beach**, on the northern end of the park.

PLANNING TIP
Always bring a hooded jacket or sweatshirt, even if sunny skies and warm weather are in the forecast. The wind chill on the Oregon Coast is no joke.

Seaside

North of Cannon Beach, Seaside is a more budget-friendly and family-oriented alternative to Cannon Beach, which generally means bigger crowds and more kids. The lively atmosphere is especially apparent at some of the seafront city's many indoor, all-weather attractions. One such attraction is **Seaside Carousel**, which features a host of whimsical creatures (including classic horses). Another is **Funland Entertainment Center**, a massive arcade complex on Broadway St with video games, pinball and an entire hall devoted to Fascination, a vintage game that

BOB POOL/SHUTTERSTOCK

reached its peak of popularity a century ago and feels like a cross between Skee-Ball and bingo.

One of the city's best-known attractions is the **Promenade** (or 'the Prom' as locals call it), which stretches alongside the coast for around 1.5 miles. It's a popular spot for a stroll; you can also rent a bicycle or a rickshaw-like Surrey cycle from **Wheel Fun Rentals** on Holladay Dr and head out for a spin. The same company also has an office at **Quatat Park** in the heart of town where you can rent kayaks, paddleboards and even swan boats to take out on the Necanicum River.

Tillamook

About 40 miles south of Cannon Beach, Tillamook is nearly synonymous with its best-known product: cheese. The city's star attraction is the **Tillamook Creamery**, which offers free self-guided experiences as well as guided cheese and ice-cream tours for those who are particularly keen on learning about cheesemaking. However, most people come with one particular destination in mind: the sample counter. Here you can try all sorts of products, from sharp cheddar to squeaky curds, free of charge. If you aren't completely cheesed out by the time you're finished at the creamery, head over to **Blue Heron French Cheese Company** a mile down the road to find even more cheese. The gourmet shop here is stocked to the gills with Blue Heron's signature brie along with all sorts of other gourmet products, and there's a candy shop in an outbuilding if you need to balance things out with a bit of sweetness. Don't miss the petting zoo, which is home to everything from pigs to llamas.

Lincoln City

If you're visiting the Oregon Coast from the Willamette Valley wine country, or if you're a fan of glass art (or kites), Lincoln City is the place to be. It's about a two-hour drive southwest of Portland

HIKING SADDLE MOUNTAIN

About 15 miles east of Seaside, Saddle Mountain offers one of the most challenging – and rewarding – hiking opportunities on the north coast. An extremely steep 2.4-mile trail leads to the mountain's 3288ft summit. While it's a challenging trek, the views from the top are worth the climb, especially on clear days, when you can see all the way to the ocean.

OREGON COAST SEAFOOD
While you'll find all sorts of seafood along the Oregon Coast, the region is best known for albacore tuna, razor clams and Dungeness crab. Razor clams are particularly prevalent in the northernmost stretch of the coast, and clam digging is a popular activity (though you'll need a permit from the Oregon Department of Fish & Wildlife to dig).

via 99W or an hour on the dot from McMinnville. The city's claims to fame include two annual kite festivals (and primo wind conditions for kite flying) as well as its large number of glass studios, including the **Lincoln City Glass Center**, where you can watch glass artists at work or try your hand behind the torch. Lincoln City's **Finders Keepers** program is another huge draw. Every year, volunteers hide around 3000 colorful glass floats crafted by artisans along the city's 7-mile stretch of coastline. If you find a float, you get to keep it. All floats have a serial number, so you can register yours online with the city's visitor bureau, **Explore Lincoln City** *(explorelincolncity.com)*, to get a certificate of authenticity and details about the artist.

Depoe Bay

A short drive south of Lincoln City, Depoe Bay is one of the best places on the Oregon Coast for whale-watching. Every summer, a group of whales spends a few months in the bay, filling up on mysid shrimp. You can learn all about them on a guided whale-watching adventure led by marine biologist Carrie Newell of **Whale Research EcoExcursions** or head to Newell's **Whale, Sea Life & Shark Museum** to check out all sorts of engaging exhibits about whales and other sea creatures.

WASHINGTON
Goonies House
Fort Stevens State Park
Astoria
Oregon Film Museum
Fort Clatsop
Gearhart
See Seaside Enlargement
Seaside
Saddle Mountain State Natural Area
PACIFIC OCEAN
Indian Beach
Ecola State Park
Ecola Point
Cannon Beach
Haystack Rock
Nehalem River
Camp 18
Seaside
3rd Ave
2nd Ave
1st Avenue
N Promenade
N Downing St
Necanicum Dr
1st Avenue
Promenade
Seaside Carousel
Quatat Park
N Holladay Dr
Broadway St
Funland Entertainment Center
Ave A
S Franklin St
Necanicum River
Wheel Fun Rentals
Ave C
0 200 m
0 0.1 miles
Neahkahnie Mountain
Nehalem
Tillamook State Forest
Manzanita
Wheeler
Jordan Creek
Bay City
Tillamook Creamery
Blue Heron French Cheese Company
Tillamook
OREGON
Cape Lookout
N Yamhill River
Nestucca River
Siuslaw National Forest
Pacific City
Grand Ronde Indian Reservation
Cascade Head
Depoe Bay
Willamina
Otis
Lincoln City
Siuslaw National Forest
Lincoln City Glass Center
Rickreall
Dallas
Gleneden Beach
Whale Research EcoExcursions
Whale, Sea Life, & Shark Museum
Monmouth
0 20 km
0 10 miles

See p136 for eating, drinking and shopping listings

Explore McMinnville

Researched by Brett Atkinson

At the heart of the Willamette Valley's wine industry lies busy and modern McMinnville. Framed by leafy neighborhoods and strung out along Hwy 99, the city has a historic, red-brick downtown precinct dating from 1890 to 1915. Look forward to exploring downtown's art galleries and boutiques, and dining and imbibing at good cafes, restaurants and wine-tasting rooms. Complementing downtown's boutique hotels are nearby wine-country stays in McMinnville's rural hinterland. Definitely spend a few days finding out why Willamette Valley pinot noir is so highly regarded, but also make time to explore a spectacular display of aviation and space history. Visit in June to celebrate the diversity of West Coast winemaking, or in May for a quirky festival focused on visitors from afar.

Getting Around

Car

Having your own vehicle or joining a guided tour is the most convenient way to explore the wine country around McMinnville.

Bus

Local services with Yamhill County Transport link McMinnville to nearby Carlton and Dayton and (slightly) further afield to Newberg.

Walking

With tasting rooms, galleries and shopping, downtown McMinnville is a great place to explore on a relaxed stroll. Carlton also offers a similar experience.

THE BEST

WINERY
Remy Wines (p131)

TASTING ROOM
Grove Tasting Room (p133)

RESTAURANT
Hayward (p136)

FESTIVAL
UFO Fest (p134)

MUSEUM EVERGREEN
Aviation & Space Museum (p134)

The Farmhouse Tasting Room, Remy Wines (p130)
ZACHARY GOFF/REMY WINES

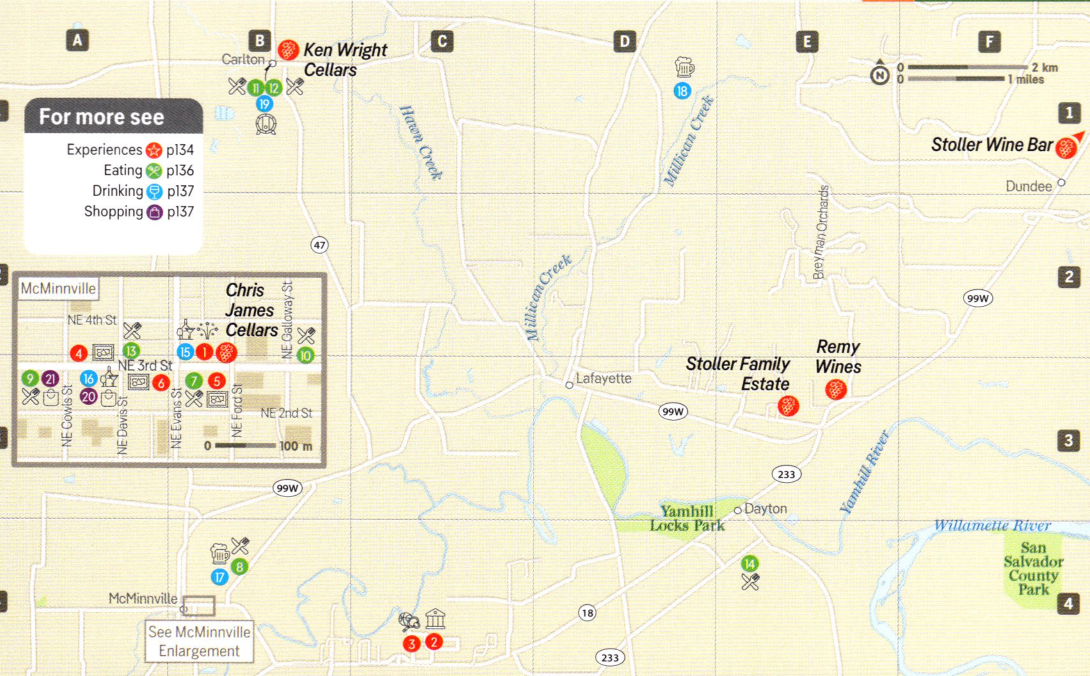

For more see
Experiences p134
Eating p136
Drinking p137
Shopping p137
Ken Wright Cellars
Carlton
Hawn Creek
Millican Creek
Stoller Wine Bar
Dundee
Breyman Orchards
Lafayette
Stoller Family Estate
Remy Wines
Yamhill River
Yamhill Locks Park
Dayton
Willamette River
San Salvador County Park
McMinnville
See McMinnville Enlargement
Chris James Cellars
NE 4th St
NE 3rd St
NE 2nd St
NE Galloway St
NE Cowls St
NE Davis St
NE Evans St
NE Ford St
0 100 m
0 2 km
0 1 miles
99W
47
233
18

★ TOP EXPERIENCE

Willamette Valley Wine Touring

The heart of wine country, McMinnville and the surrounding region showcase many of the Willamette Valley's vineyards and wineries. Carlton, 7 miles north of McMinnville, and Dayton, 7 miles to the east, also feature vineyards and tasting rooms perfect for sampling world-beating pinot noir.

MAP **P131**

The Willamette Valley's Wine Country

Oregon's first wineries were established elsewhere in the 1850s, and it wasn't until the 1960s and 1970s that the winemaking potential of the Willamette Valley was fully recognized. Around McMinnville, Newberg and Dundee, the northern Willamette Valley's mild climate and long summers foster the delicate pinot noir grape, as well as significant plantings of pinot gris, chardonnay and riesling. In the broader Willamette Valley AVA (American Viticultural Area), there are now more than 700 wineries scattered across 11 different sub-region AVAs.

Planning a Visit

Most vineyards and tasting rooms are open year-round, and high season is from June to October. Weekends and holidays can be very busy with day visitors heading south from Portland, so for a more relaxed and intimate vineyard experience, consider visiting on a weekday. Some vineyards and tastings open daily, while from around noon to 5pm from Wednesday to Sunday is the norm for others. Double-check opening hours before setting off.

PLANNING TIP
Visit the Chamber of Commerce in McMinnville for maps, tips and information on wineries and other attractions in the area before heading out. Open Monday to Friday.

Scan for information.

PERNELLE VOYAGE/SHUTTERSTOCK

Tasting-Room Protocol

Depending on the vintages and wine styles offered, the cost of a curated and guided wine tasting is from $20 to $70. These costs are usually waived or discounted if you purchase wine at the vineyard or join its wine club. Prior reservation for tastings is preferred by most vineyards and tasting rooms, but walk-ins for couples and smaller groups is usually OK based on availability. Unlike other US wine regions like Napa and Sonoma, the Willamette Valley is more focused on smaller, family-owned vineyards and boutique wineries. At the smallest vineyard tasting rooms, there's a good chance you'll be attended to by the actual winemaker. With hundreds of vineyards in the region, try to focus a visit on three at most. You'll have more time to relax – maybe enjoying a picnic or a snack platter – and enjoy the wines.

QUICK BREAK
Refuel and relax at the compact gathering of food trucks at **Mac Plaza**. Mexican flavors are the shared focus just south of downtown McMinnville. Check out @macplazaor on Instagram.

Relaxed Rural Vineyards

Highlights of the vineyards around McMinnville include **Remy Wines** *(remywines.com)*. It's housed in a vintage farmhouse in the Dundee Hills and is the perfect location at which winemaker, and former mayor of McMinnville, Remy Drabkin can craft single-vineyard, single-varietal Italian wines. The relaxed bucolic location also hosts the annual Queer Wine Fest (p166) in late June.

A short drive west on McDougall Rd is **Stoller Family Estate** *(stollerfamilyestate.com;* pictured), leaders in promoting sustainable wine-growing practices in the region, and the world's first LEED Gold Certified winery guaranteeing sustainability and environmentally friendly design. Take in superb views from the spectacular 4000-sq-ft tasting room and book ahead for summer Lawn Experiences including frosé (frozen rosé) and a picnic. Opened in March 2025, the popular **Stoller Wine Bar** in Newberg serves seasonal shared plates from an on-site food truck.

Downtown Tasting Rooms

If you're short of time, you don't need to visit the vineyards to sip local wines. Downtown McMinnville, and also the nearby towns of Carlton and Dayton, offer tasting rooms perfect to explore on a relaxed stroll. In McMinnville, secure a spot on the sunny patio at **Chris James Cellars** *(chrisjames cellars.com)* and enjoy wines from the Willamette Valley and across the Columbia River in Washington. Award-winning wines harnessing Italian dolcetto and Spanish tempranillo grapes prove the region's diverse terroir supports more than just pinot noir and chardonnay. In nearby Carlton, the tasting room for **Ken Wright Cellars** *(kenwright cellars.com)* is in the town's heritage 1920s train depot. Tastings provide a definitive overview of local pinot noir from this well-established winery.

THANKSGIVING
Many Willamette Valley wineries celebrate Thanksgiving (November) with two weekends of rare-wine tastings, food, wine-matching events and live music.

WINE CONCIERGE
Paul Beck – aka the **Willamette Wine Concierge** *(willamette wineconcierge.com)* – arranges curated food and wine itineraries, either guided or self-drive.

Walk Downtown McMinnville

Stroll McMinnville's historic downtown precinct, enjoying excellent food, beer and wine, and browsing in an eclectic range of shops reflecting the best of small-town America. If you wish to include winery tasting rooms in your walk, schedule a weekend visit as that's when most will be open.

START	END	LENGTH
Alchemist's Jam & Bakery	Thistle	1 mile; two hours

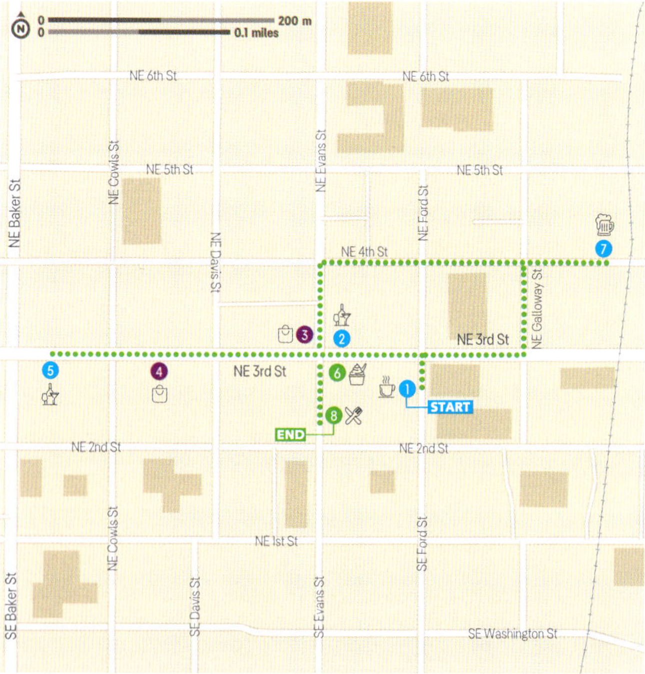

1 Coffee & Oven-Fresh Baking

Begin the day at **Alchemist's Jam & Bakery** for McMinnville's best coffee and morning buns served straight from the oven. Arrive early for the best selection. There's also house-made jams and preserves, and fresh sourdough loaves for picnics.

2 Retro Hotel & Rooftop Bar

Originally opened as the Hotel Eberton in 1905, **McMenamins Hotel Oregon** (p139) is downtown McMinnville's tallest building, and the brick edifice is a fine example of Richardsonian Romanesque architecture. Pop inside to check out the hotel's quirky decor, and ask if any live music is scheduled for the rooftop bar.

3 Wine, Gifts & More

Cross the street to **NW Food and Gifts** for items sourced from around the Willamette Valley and Pacific Northwest. There's a strong focus on all things edible, including chocolate and confectionery, and more than 160 local wines. Gift hampers are good for indecisive shoppers.

4 Hit the Books

Continue west along Third St to the eponymous independent bookshop. With scores of fiction and non-fiction titles from around the region, **Third Street Books** is the kind of place you'd love to have in your own hometown.

5 Organic, Sustainable & Biodynamic Wine

It's just 100yd to the **Grove Tasting Room**, the shared downtown hub of local vineyards Montinore Estates and Landline Estates. Sample the estates' surprising wines in the Grove's elegant brick-lined space. Lunch snacks include tinned Spanish seafood and local cheese and charcuterie.

6 Vintage Ice-Cream Parlor

Return east along Third St for a sweet treat at **Serendipity Ice Cream**. This 19th-century-style parlor is in the former Cook's Hotel built in 1886. Check out the player (self-playing) piano doing its thing in the corner.

7 Rustic Brewery

Time for a beer at **ForeLand Beer**, a hyper-local taproom popular with regulars enjoying easy-drinking lagers and IPAs, often released on a seasonal basis. If you're traveling with a well-behaved dog, you should feel right at home.

8 Casual Fine Dining

Adjourn for a leisurely evening meal at **Thistle**, equal parts neighborhood bar and fine-dining bistro. The chalkboard menu changes on a daily basis, but you're guaranteed local and seasonal ingredients. Excellent cocktails, too.

EXPERIENCES

Drink in the Diversity of the Queer Wine Festival

FESTIVAL

First held in 2022, June's annual **Queer Wine Fest** *(queerwinefest.com)* attracts LGBTIQ+ winemakers, mainly from around California and the Pacific Northwest.

Highlights of the one-day festival held at **Remy Wines** *(remywines.com)* east of McMinnville in Dayton include outdoor tastings and live music. Vineyard owner and winemaker Remy Drabkin is also an LGBTIQ+ community advocate and was mayor of McMinnville from 2022 to 2024.

Another popular McMinnville wine festival is the annual **International Pinot Noir Festival** *(ipnc.org)* held for three days at Linfield University in late July. The festival took a break in 2025, but was expected to return in 2026.

Don't Stop Believing at UFO Fest

FESTIVAL

MAP: 1 P131 B2

Back in 1950, a farmer from nearby Sheridan reckoned he saw a UFO – relatively convincing photos were published in *Life* magazine – and since 1999, McMinnville has celebrated with May's annual **UFO Fest** *(ufofest.com)*. Some visitors are in town to attend serious lectures and presentations from authoritative guest speakers, but for most folk it's all about the UFO-themed concerts and the end-of-festival Alien Costume Ball. The popular Alien Pet Costume Contest sees a mixed feline and canine crew of good boys and good girls dressed up in a veritable galaxy of get-ups. The annual Alien Costume parade down Third St is also an interplanetary marvel. Events are held around downtown and at McMenamins Hotel Oregon.

Discover Aviation & Space History at Evergreen

MUSEUM

MAP: 2 P131 C4

Look for the Boeing 747, and you're in the right place. Actually, it's very hard to miss the **Evergreen Aviation & Space Museum** *(evergreenmuseum.org; adult/child $24/14)*, 3 miles east of downtown McMinnville. As well as a jumbo jet parked up in a roadside paddock, there's a whole squadron of historic fighter jets on display outside, and two huge hangars filled with airplanes, helicopters and other assorted flying machines.

Dominating the Aviation hangar is the *Spruce Goose,* a massive flying boat envisioned and built by the eccentric business tycoon, Howard Hughes. Don't miss taking a guided tour of the *Spruce Goose*'s cockpit. Dozens of other restored and replica aircraft also feature, and military planes are particularly well represented.

Across the car park in Evergreen's leviathan Space hangar, exhibits include a Titan II rocket used in NASA's Gemini Program, a super-sleek SR-71 Blackbird spy plane, and a menacing F-117 Nighthawk stealth bomber. The museum is (deservedly) very popular, so visiting when it first opens at 9am is recommended.

Cool Off at the Evergreen Wings & Waves Waterpark

WATER PARK

MAP: 3 P131 **C4**

A McMinnville must during summer, this indoor **water park** *(wingsandwaveswaterpark.com; admission $39, children under two free)* next to the aviation museum is equally unmissable, with another Boeing 747 perched on its roof. Inside are 10 waterslides (including four that come out of the 747), a wave pool, a leisure pool and a pool for toddlers. Plenty of lifeguards keep everyone safe, and yes, that is a space shuttle beside one of the waterslides.

BEST DOWNTOWN GALLERIES

Sampling wine at downtown tasting rooms and browsing local art galleries is a perfect McMinnville combo.

John Stromme Art Gallery

Bold acrylics often referencing nature and heritage themes. Other local artists are also consistently featured. John is usually keen for a chat.

MAP: 4 P131 **A2**

Currents Gallery

Fine arts and crafts from more than 60 Oregon artists, with work covering every medium from painting and printmaking to jewelry and ceramics.

MAP: 5 P131 **B3**

Artemis Fox Gallery

Stunning screen prints depicting Oregon landscapes and prints on wood of local wildlife and scenery. Also jewelry and illustrated children's books.

MAP: 6 P131 **A3**

THE LEGENDARY SPRUCE GOOSE

Originally envisioned as a long-range troop carrier for WWII, the *Spruce Goose* – aka the Hughes H-4 Hercules – is still the world's largest wood-framed airplane. Finally completed in 1947, with Hughes at the wheel the airplane flew for just under a mile at Long Beach before being hangared indefinitely in California. It was moved to McMinnville in 1993 and reassembled to go on display in 2001. See the Martin Scorsese film, *The Aviator* (2004) for the incredible *Spruce Goose* saga.

LISTINGS

Best Places for...

$ Budget $$ Midrange $$$ Top End

Eating

Breakfast

Crescent Cafe $$
7 B3
Cozy and welcoming spot on McMinnville's Third St for a leisurely breakfast. Ease into the day with apple pecan crepes or hearty eggs with corn-beef hash. Lunch features salads and sandwiches. Expect a short wait for a table at weekend brunch. *crescentcafeonthird.com; 7:30am-2pm Wed-Mon*

Casual Dining

Mac Market $
8 B4
Industrial-style shared space half a mile northeast of downtown in McMinnville's former granary district. Highlights include wood-fired pizza from Honey Pie and excellent coffee and baked goods at Bodhi Bakery. *macmkt.com; 8am-7pm Tue-Sun*

Abuela's Nuestra Cocina 
9 A3
Well-priced Mexican restaurant on Third St with a menu focused around the traditional recipes of the owners, the Fernandez family. Try the complex *mole poblano* or team a few street tacos with a deceptively strong margarita. *abuelasnuestracocina.com; 11:30am-8pm Mon-Sat*

Wine Bars

HiFi Wine Bar $$
10 B2
Food, wine and music with locally inspired shared plates paired with weekend live gigs and vintage jazz vinyl. Classy and cosmopolitan in McMinnville. *hifiwinebar.com; 2-10pm Wed-Fri, from 1pm Sat & Sun*

Horse Radish 
11 B1
Relaxed hybrid of wine bar and restaurant with artisan cheese plates, gourmet sandwiches and tasty comfort food. Located in nearby Carlton with live music on Saturday nights. Sunday brunch is popular. *thehorseradish.com; 11:30am-2pm Mon-Thu, to 8pm Fri & Sat, 10:30am-3pm Sun*

Fine Dining

Hayward $$$
12 B1
Innovative fine dining in downtown Carlton. James Beard Award–nominated chef Kari Shaughnessy harnesses local Oregon produce on a menu seamlessly blending Japanese, European and Pacific Northwest influences. *haywardrestaurant.com; 5-9pm Wed-Sat*

Humble Spirit $$$
13 A2
Elevated comfort food enhanced by ingredients sourced from local farms and producers. Book ahead for weekend brunch. Next door is the more casual Humble Spirit pub with slow-smoked barbecue. *humblespirit.love; 4:30-9pm Thu-Mon, 9am-2pm Sat & Sun*

Joel Palmer House $$$

 E4

Known for its dishes built around wild mushrooms and Oregon truffles, this elegant restaurant is 7 miles east of McMinnville in Dayton. Tasting menus begin at five-course experiences. Reservations essential. *joelpalmerhouse.com; 5-9pm Tue-Sat*

Drinking

Bars

McMenamins Hotel Oregon

15 B2

Look forward to 360-degree views from the rooftop bar crowning McMinnville's tallest building. The food, including burgers and sandwiches, can be hit and miss, but elevated vistas and good beer, wine and cocktails make it worth a visit. *mcmenamins.com/hotel-oregon; noon-9pm Mon-Thu, to 11pm Fri-Sun*

Blue Moon Lounge

 A3

Formerly a 1920s soda shop, Blue Moon Lounge became a bar at the end of Prohibition. It's now reckoned to be the longest continually operating bar in McMinnville's Yamhill County, with locals crowding in for beer and cocktails, and hearty food like wings, steak and burgers. Definitely fire up the jukebox. *bluemoonmac.com; 7am-2:30am*

Craft Beer

Heater Allen Brewing

17 B4

Renowned for crafting some of Oregon's best German- and Czech-style lagers. Enjoy the brewery's award-winning beers with pizza or pasta from the on-site Brassi's food truck. *heaterallen.com; 4-8pm Mon, Thu & Fri, 1-8pm Sat & Sun*

Root & Rye Hop Farm and Brewery

 D1

Well-crafted beers served on the outskirts of Carlton. Standout brews include the Misty Mountain IPA. There's a yard full of fun games, including shuffleboard, cornhole, darts and pickleball. *rootnrye.com; noon-7:30pm Wed-Sun*

Spirits

Bull Run Distillery

 B1

Willamette Valley outpost of Portland's Bull Run Distillery, with whiskey, bourbon and vodka on offer at its Carlton tasting room. Also has a compact section selling gifts and artisan products sourced from around the Willamette Valley. *bullrundistillery.com; noon-6pm Fri-Sun*

Shopping

Music

Vortex

 A3

Brilliant independent record shop with overflowing bins of new and used vinyl and a big range of band posters, T-shirts and merch. Check the front window for listings of local gigs. *facebook.com/thevortexrecords; 11am-6pm Wed-Sun*

Vintage

Vintage on Third

 A3

Curated collections of vintage fashion, design and homewares. Where to head if you're after retro 1960s glass design, vintage tin toys and eclectic examples of objet d'art. *vintageonthird.com; 11am-5pm*

See p145
for eating,
drinking and
shopping
listings

Explore Newberg & Dundee

Researched by Brett Atkinson

Alternative gateways to Willamette Valley wine country, the small cities of Newberg and Dundee are a few miles apart along Hwy 99. Echoes of the region's Quaker and settler heritage linger in local museums and historic sites, but the towns' contemporary look is now more about traffic, strip malls and essential modern services. Dotted with heritage buildings, Newberg's historic downtown district is bisected by busy Hwy 99, and the surrounding rural hinterland is full of superb vineyards and characterful places to sleep. Great eating and excellent craft beer abounds, and the interesting final stop on the challenging Oregon Trail makes for a good day trip or a convenient sightseeing stop when heading south from Portland.

Getting Around

Car

Your own vehicle is best for exploring around Newberg and Dundee. From Portland it's around 25 miles to Newberg. Visiting Oregon City on route adds around 15 miles.

Bus

Caravan Shuttle links Portland International Airport with Newberg and Dundee. Local bus services on Yamhill County Transport link Newberg and Dundee with McMinnville.

Tour

A guided vineyard tour is a great way to get around Willamette Valley wine country, especially if you're traveling in a group.

THE BEST

WINERY
Ambar Estate (p142)

BREWERY
Wolves & People Farmhouse Brewery (p144)

RETRO CINEMA
99W Drive-In (p144)

MUSEUM
Hoover-Minthorn House (p143)

HISTORY EXPERIENCE
Champoeg State Heritage Area (p143)

Yurt, Champoeg State Heritage Area (p143)
DOUGLAS H. ORTON/ALAMY

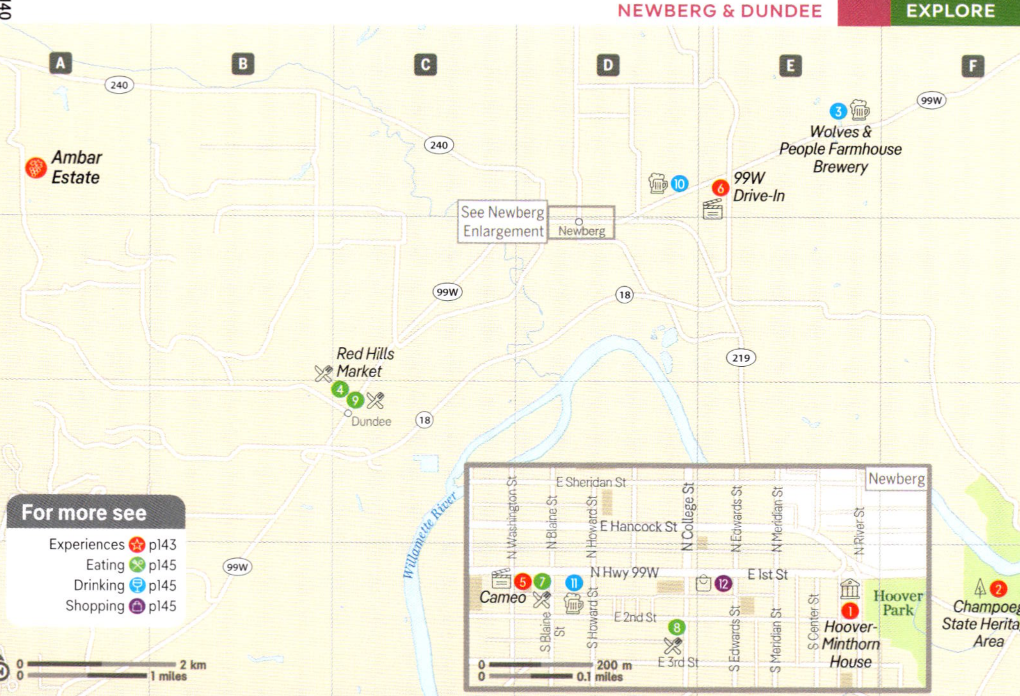
Ambar Estate
240
99W
18
219
Wolves & People Farmhouse Brewery
99W Drive-In
See Newberg Enlargement
Newberg
Red Hills Market
Dundee
Willamette River
Champoeg State Heritage Area
Newberg
E Sheridan St
E Hancock St
N Hwy 99W
E 1st St
E 2nd St
E 3rd St
N Washington St
N Blaine St
N Howard St
N College St
N Edwards St
N Meridian St
N River St
S Blaine St
S Howard St
S Edwards St
S Meridian St
S Center St
Cameo
Hoover Park
Hoover-Minthorn House
0 200 m
0 0.1 miles
0 2 km
0 1 miles
For more see
Experiences p143
Eating p145
Drinking p145
Shopping p145

★ TOP EXPERIENCE

Wine Touring Around Newberg & Dundee

Featuring the most established vineyards of the Willamette Valley, the gentle folds of the Chehalem Mountains and Dundee Hills also conceal several spectacular places ideal for a leisurely wine-country lunch. Look forward to pairing delicious food with some of the world's finest pinot noir.

MAP P140

Two Renowned AVAs

Encompassing the **Chehalem Mountains** and **Dundee Hills** AVAs (American Viticultural Areas), the wine-growing region around Newberg and Dundee is especially renowned for pinot noir, but chardonnay and pinot gris are also important. The Dundee Hills is the valley's most intensely farmed vineyard area, and where the region's first grapes were planted in 1965.

Named after its owners, Rollin and Corby Soles, Newberg's **Roco Winery** *(rocowinery.com)* specializes in pinot noir, chardonnay and sparkling wines, while its rosé wines are ideal for warmer days.

Established in 1971, **Adelsheim Vineyard** *(adelsheim.com)* combines superb pinot noir and chardonnay with Chehalem Mountains views, and both grape varieties are also harnessed for their Blanc de Blancs sparkling wines.

PLANNING TIP

Operators offering private and customized tours around local wineries include Oregon Select Wine Tours, Valley Vineyard Tours and Grape Escape Tours. If exploring independently, nominate a designated driver.

Food & Wine Experiences

Unlike wine regions in Australia, South Africa and New Zealand, Willamette Valley vineyards don't usually offer restaurant dining. Most provide snacks or shared platters including cheese and

DAVID KRUG/ALAMY

charcuterie, and many offer outdoor areas ideal for an alfresco picnic. Stock up on picnic fixings at Dundee's Red Hills Market (p144).

Wineries that do offer lunches include **Domaine Willamette** *(domainewillamette.com)* in the Dundee Hills, where *méthode traditionnelle* sparkling wines are partnered with a bistro menu including wild mushroom crab cakes, lamb ragout and steak frites. Closed Monday and Tuesday.

To the northwest closer to Carlton, **Soter Vineyards** *(sotervineyards.com)* serves a seven-course lunch tasting menu (per person $150) at its Mineral Springs Ranch tasting room. Reservations essential. Soter is known for biodynamic pinot noir and chardonnay.

With a Dundee Hills tasting room spanning Japanese gardens and two minimalist pavilions, **Ambar Estate** *(ambarestate.com)* is the Willamette Valley's first certified regenerative organic vineyard. Book ahead to pair award-winning pinot noir and chardonnay with a five-course menu of shared plates (per person $125).

EXPERIENCES

Learn about Presidential History at Hoover-Minthorn House

MUSEUM

MAP: 1 P140 E4

The Pacific Northwest's only presidential house museum, **Hoover-Minthorn House** (*hooverminthorn.org; adult/child $7.50/5;* pictured left) is where Herbert Hoover (the 31st president of the USA) lived from 1885 to 1891. Built in 1881 by Jesse Edwards, the Quaker founder of Newberg, the home later became the residence of Hoover's uncle, Dr Henry Minthorn, and the restored home is now a museum of period furnishings and early Oregon history.

After becoming an orphan in 1884, Hoover was 10 years old when be headed west from Iowa, and his six-year stay with his uncle's family in Newberg transitioned him to adolescence and independence. The Willamette Valley remained important to him, and he visited Newberg several times during his presidency from 1929 to 1933.

The house museum is usually open from Thursday to Sunday, but phone ahead to confirm.

Explore the Champoeg State Heritage Area

HISTORIC SITE

MAP: 2 P140 F4

Around 6 miles southeast of Newberg, the **Champoeg State Heritage Area** (*stateparks.oregon.gov*) is a popular family destination with 15 acres of old-growth woodland, grassy meadows, nature trails, historic sites, campgrounds and a playground.

In the 1840s the town was contemplating a positive future with a steamboat landing, stagecoach office and a granary, and during the administrative vacuum when the status of the Oregon Territory was disputed by the United States and the United Kingdom, the good people of Champoeg voted to establish the first provisional American government on the Pacific Coast.

Films and displays in the museum outline the events leading to to 1843's famous vote, and there are also exhibits on the region's indigenous Kalapuya people. In 1861, less than 20 years after the empire-challenging vote, Champoeg was abandoned after devastating floods.

ENJOY A NEWBERG FRIDAY NIGHT

On the first Friday of every month – excluding January and July – Newberg's downtown precinct is enlivened by the **Newberg Art Walk**. Events run from 5pm to 8pm with galleries, makers and artists displaying their work. Some art is displayed in wine-tasting rooms, and there's also live music. See newberg_art_walk on Instagram for details.

Enjoy Craft Beer at Wolves & People

BREWERY

MAP: 3 P140 E1

There's no shortage of fine wine around Newberg, but with **Wolves & People Farmhouse Brewery** *(wolvesandpeople.com)* the town also features one of Oregon's most interesting craft breweries.

Located just north of Newberg on his family's hazelnut farm, Christian DeBenedetti, a beer writer, bluegrass musician and brewer, crafts barrel-aged and wild-fermented beers infused with the local terroir of the Willamette Valley. The brewery is stationed in the farm's former hazelnut-packing shed, and seasonal brews could include a tart dry-hopped saison or a lush stout made with white truffles.

A tasting flight is the best way to explore Wolves & People's invention and diversity. Follow @wolvesand-people on Instagram to see what's currently on tap, and look forward to bluegrass music most Thursday nights from 6pm. Either secure a table in the rustic taproom or pull up an Adirondack chair around the fire pit. Open from 4pm to 9pm on Thursdays, from 3pm on Fridays, and 1pm on Saturday and Sunday.

Feast on Local Produce at Red Hills Market

DELI/MARKET

MAP: 4 P140 C3

The dining scene around Newberg and Dundee spans every occasion, from finely crafted degustation menus to Modern American bistros, but one of the region's standout eateries is actually a relaxed combination of deli, grocery and market. Local gourmet produce is for sale at **Red Hills Market** *(redhillsmarket.com; 8am to 8pm)*, but most folk are here for the artisan sandwiches made with rustic artisan bread or equally good wood-fired pizza. Select a beer from the taplist showcasing local craft breweries and retire to the rear patio for a quintessential Dundee experience. There's also apartment accommodations on-site at the **Market Lofts** *(themarketlofts.com)*.

DON'T FORGET THE POPCORN

Welcome to Oregon's hub for retro movie-going. For three generations, Newberg's Francis family have owned the town's historic cinema. The same family operates the town drive-in. See what's screening at both venues on 99w.com.

Cameo

MAP: 5 P140 D4

Located on Newberg's main street, this historic cinema first opened in 1937, and still retains many original art deco design features.

99W Drive-In

MAP: 6 P140 E1

Opened in 1953, the drive-in screens movies on Friday, Saturday and Sunday nights from early May to late October.

LISTINGS

Best Places for...

$ Budget $$ Midrange $$$ Top End

Eating

Barbecue

Storrs Smokehouse $$

Southern-style BBQ on Newberg's main drag with brisket, pulled pork, ribs and wings. The Gran' Daddy Try 'Em All plate is ideal for two (hungry) diners. Slather on the Oregon pinot noir BBQ sauce. *storrssmokehouse.com; 11am-7pm Wed-Sun*

Bistro Style

Painted Lady $$$

Eight-course tasting menus shine showcased in a gracious 1890s Victorian home in Newberg. Wine matches are Oregon-focused and local and seasonal ingredients are consistently featured. *thepaintedladyrestaurant.com; 5-10pm Thu-Sat*

Tina's $$$

In Dundee, this intimate French-influenced bistro showcases lamb, rabbit and duck to perfection, and seafood often stars on the menu of starters. Expect organic and seasonal ingredients and an exemplary local wine list. Reservations recommended. *tinasdundee.com; 5-9pm Wed-Sun*

Drinking

Craft Beer & Cocktails

Stumptown Taps

10 D1

Hoppy heaven with 20 taps from the best of Portland and Oregon breweries to finds from other West Coast heavy hitters. *stumptowntaps.com; noon-8pm Sun, 2-10pm Mon-Thu, noon-10pm Fri & Sat*

Barley & Vine Tavern

11 D4

Newberg favorite with 16 beer taps, plus a savvy wine and cocktail list. The food menu serves up gourmet pizza, wellness bowls and bar snacks. *barleyandvinetavern.com; 2-10pm Mon-Thu, from noon Fri & Sat*

Shopping

Food

Red Hills Market

see 4

Versatile Dundee deli-market with artisan gourmet produce showcasing the Willamette Valley. Top spot for picnic and BBQ fixings. *redhillsmarket.com; 8am-8pm*

Vintage & Apparel

Velour

12 E4

Americana folk meets Pacific Northwest heritage at Newberg's Velour, an aesthetic-forward lifestyle shop curating vintage and handmade clothing, jewelry and accessories. *shopvelour.com; 10am-6pm Thu-Sun*

★ WORTH A TRIP

Oregon City

The final stop on the arduous Oregon Trail, and the first US city founded west of the Rockies, Oregon City combines a charming historic precinct with a quirky urban elevator, and the immense white-water spectacle of the Willamette Falls. Don't miss the excellent regional museum.

GETTING THERE
Oregon City is about 25 miles east of Newberg. Alternatively, stop by when heading south from Portland, around 15 miles north. Via Hwy 99 is a scenic route.

Oregon City Elevator

Oregon City was initially built at river level, but as it grew, development moved up the cliffs facing the Willamette River. A rickety water-powered elevator to link the 'lower' and 'upper' towns went into service in 1915. Passengers had to climb out a trap door and up a ladder when it (frequently) stopped working. The more reliable **Oregon City Elevator** *(free;* pictured) dates from the 1950s, and is one of only four municipal elevators in the world. There's convenient parking at the base of the elevator and excellent views of the Willamette Falls when you ascend. Ask at the volunteer-staffed counter on the upper level for a walking map of the nearby McLoughlin Historic District.

McLoughlin Historic District

Built by one of Oregon's founding fathers, John McLoughlin, the 1845 **McLoughlin House** *(mcloughlinhouse.org)* is reached via a clifftop path from the elevator. On Fridays and Saturdays, free guided tours of the clapboard home – considered a mansion when most locals lived in log cabins – begin next door at Barclay House.

Around 400yd from McLoughlin House, **Stevens-Crawford Heritage House** *(clackamashistory.org; adult/child $8/5)* offers more insight into

Scan this QR code for Oregon City info.

AN DEWAR PHOTOGRAPHY/SHUTTERSTOCK

the town's settler history. Owned by a pioneering family, the 1908 house boasts original furniture, plus innovative (at the time) electric light fixtures, indoor plumbing and central heating. Open Thursday to Saturday.

Museum of the Oregon Territory

From Wednesday to Sunday, this excellent **museum** *(clackamashistory.org; adult/child $8/5)* features the region's Native American heritage and pioneer history, and also galleries on the horseshoe-shaped **Willamette Falls**, at 1500ft-wide and 40m-high the biggest by volume in the Pacific Northwest. Head to the 2nd floor for views of the surging falls, the source of, hydro-electricity powering Portland from 1889 and also the now-abandoned paper mills nearby.

QUICK BREAK
A retro American diner, **Mike's Drive In** is ideal for a quick meal. Mushrooms, jalapeño peppers, blue cheese and bacon are all optional burger toppings.

See p156
for eating,
drinking and
shopping
listings

Explore Salem

Researched by Brett Atkinson

A relaxed university city that, as Oregon's state capital, is imbued with a slightly conservative ambience, Salem is a convenient base for exploring more interesting destinations nearby. After admiring the bold architecture of the Oregon State Capitol and learning about the region's Native American heritage at an excellent museum and gallery, hit the trails for superb waterfall views at a spectacular state park, or wander on manicured pathways through a beautiful themed garden. Slightly further afield, the European pedigree of a nearby town is reflected by a hilltop abbey, a traditional brewery and a popular beer festival. Just an hour's drive from Portland, Salem makes for a good day trip, and it's also only 40 minutes from the heart of the Willamette Valley's wine country.

Getting Around

Walking

The best way to explore downtown Salem, especially Riverfront Park and around the Oregon State Capitol.

Car

Having your own vehicle is recommended to explore around the city. Silver Falls State Park is worthy of its own day trip, while Mt Angel and the Oregon Garden can be combined on a day-long adventure.

Bus

Direct buses travel from Salem's Downtown Transit Center to Mt Angel, but for the Oregon Garden you'll need to transfer en route.

THE BEST

HISTORIC BUILDING
Oregon State Capitol (p153)

WATERFALL
South Falls (p152)

ARCHITECTURE
Gordon House (p151)

GARDENS
Oregon Garden (p151)

FAMILY FUN
Albany Carousel (p155)

Oregon State Capitol
BOB POOL/SHUTTERSTOCK

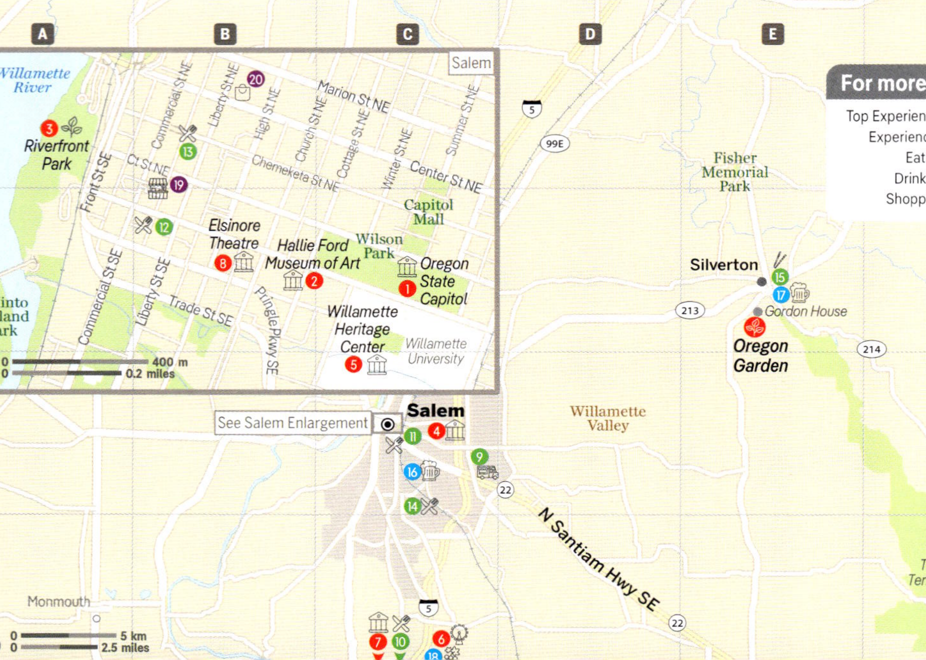
Salem
Willamette River
Riverfront Park
Minto Island Park
Front St SE
Commercial St NE
Liberty St NE
High St NE
Church St NE
Cottage St NE
Winter St NE
Summer St NE
Marion St NE
Center St NE
Chemeketa St NE
Ct St NE
Capitol Mall
Elsinore Theatre
Hallie Ford Museum of Art
Wilson Park
Oregon State Capitol
Commercial St SE
Liberty St SE
Trade St SE
Pringle Pkwy SE
Willamette Heritage Center
Willamette University
400 m
0.2 miles
See Salem Enlargement
Salem
Fisher Memorial Park
Silverton
Gordon House
Oregon Garden
Willamette Valley
N Santiam Hwy SE
South Falls
North Falls
Trail of Ten Falls
Silver Falls State Park
Monmouth
5 km
2.5 miles
For more see
Top Experiences p151
Experiences p153
Eating p156
Drinking p157
Shopping p157

★ TOP EXPERIENCE

The Oregon Garden

Opened in 1999, the Oregon Garden features more than 20 specialty garden environments across 80 acres. Year-round, the ambience of the gardens evolves across the seasons. Late May through to early July is the most colorful time, with thousands of bright and vibrant floral blooms.

Stroll Through Nature

From the **visitor center** *(oregongarden.org; adult/child $14/7)*, navigate to the Water Gardens to say hi to 'Mr Ed,' a sea serpent sculpture that wouldn't be out place in a certain Scottish loch.

Lined with maple trees, the nearby **Bosque** is especially vibrant during fall, while the **Conifer Garden** features a pleasantly confounding trail around conifers and evergreen trees sourced from the world. The grove offers a fascinating insight into the diversity of the planet's conifer species. Further on, to the left of the Oregon Garden Resort's elevated location, the **Rediscovery Forest** features managed and unmanaged acreage, not to mention raccoons, black-tailed deer and woodpeckers. Check the garden's website for details of spring and summer tram tours and other events, including art shows and yoga sessions.

PLANNING TIP
Overlooking the gardens, Oregon Garden Resort features comfortable rooms, a cozy fireside lounge and a garden-view restaurant. Also on-site is the Moonstone Spa.

A Surprising Home

Just off the driveway into the garden is the **Gordon House** *(thegordonhouse.org; adult/child $20/5)*, the only building in Oregon designed by Frank Lloyd Wright. The house was moved to its present location in 2002. Designed in 1957 and built in 1963, its organic design and open-plan format hints at a far more contemporary provenance. Check opening hours and book guided tours online.

Scan for info on visiting the garden.

★ TOP EXPERIENCE

Silver Falls State Park

An easy day trip 26 miles east of Salem, Silver Falls State Park is reached via winding forested roads. Brilliant short walks and longer hiking experiences offer superb waterfall views, and camping, swimming, biking and horseback riding are also popular activities.

PLANNING TIP
Try to avoid visiting on a spring or summer weekend or around public holidays when the car parks and most popular trails will be very busy.

North vs South?

The **North Falls** and **South Falls** are absolute highlights of visiting the park. Departing from near a new car park opened in late 2024, the North Falls Lookout trail is a 1-mile return walk for views of the 136ft-high waterfall. Don't miss continuing behind the falls.

Departing from the larger South Falls parking area, the South Falls are even more spectacular. Thundering over a mossy ledge to a rocky pool 177ft below, the waterfalls are best viewed on the trail down. Expect to be drenched by cool mist before also thrillingly continuing on right behind the falls.

A 10 Waterfall Adventure

Silver Falls' most famous experience is the **Trail of Ten Falls**, a relatively easy 7.2-mile loop trail that winds up a narrow basalt canyon and through thick Douglas fir forests framed by ferns, moss and wildflowers. As per the trail's name, hikers get to experience 10 different cascades, and through the canyon section of the trail there's the opportunity to walk behind four of the rushing torrents. Several of the waterfalls along the trail are more than 100ft high, and in summer walkers cool off in swimming holes.

Scan this QR code for park info.

EXPERIENCES

Admire the State Capitol

HISTORIC BUILDING

MAP: 1 P150 C2

Visible on the skyline right across downtown Salem, the **Oregon State Capitol** *(oregoncapitol.com)* was built in 1938 after the destruction by fire of former capitol buildings in 1855 and 1935. The current edifice combines art deco and Bauhaus design influences, especially the strident bas-relief in the front statuary and the hatbox-like cupola. Atop the cupola is the **Oregon Pioneer**, aka the 'Gold Man,' a 23ft-tall bronze statue painted with 11oz of gold leaf. The exterior of the building is faced with white Vermont marble while the interior is lined with rose travertine quarried in Montana.

A multi-year seismic retrofit project costing almost $600 million was expected to be completed by early 2026. Check the website for details of guided tours and the building's reopening. At the time of writing, virtual tours of the building were available online. Framing the capitol, Wilson Park – part of the larger State Capitol State Park – is enlivened by cherry blossoms in early spring.

Learn about Indigenous History at the Hallie Ford Museum of Art

ART & CULTURE

MAP: 2 P150 B2

Renowned as one of the finest private art collections in the Pacific Northwest, this **gallery** *(hfma.willamette.edu; adult/child $8/free)* adjoins Salem's liberal-arts-focused Willamette University. A highlight of the boxy International Style building completed in 1965 is the **Confederated Tribes of the Grand Ronde Gallery**, with Indigenous baskets, bags and ceremonial attire displayed alongside contemporary works from Native American artists. Closed Sunday and Monday.

Explore Riverfront Park

RIVERSIDE RAMBLE

MAP: 3 P150 A1

Escape downtown Salem's commercial grid by exploring the

SALEM'S SAKURA SEASON

Held across the last two weeks of March, Salem's cherry-blossom festival celebrates Japanese culture, art and food. The festival commences on **Cherry Blossom Day** on the third Saturday of the month, with Japanese lanterns being hung amid the pastel-colored blooms of the trees lining the pedestrian pathways of Wilson Park. It's a spectacular and moving display – especially after dark – and Salem is frequently ranked as one of the world's top cities to view springtime *sakura* (cherry blossoms). Follow @oregonstatecapitol on Instagram for Bloom Watch updates on the flowers' arrival.

OSH MUSEUM OF MENTAL HEALTH

The Oregon State Hospital first opened as a psychiatric institution in 1883, and more than 140 years later it still provides support to Oregonians needing psychiatric care. The filming location for the movie version of the novel *One Flew Over the Cuckoo's Nest* by the late Oregon author Ken Kesey, the hospital also houses the very moving **OSH Museum of Mental Health** *(oshmuseum.org; adult/child $7/free)*.

The evolution of psychiatric treatments across the decades is covered in fascinating and poignant detail, and there's a gallery with insights, props and artifacts from the filming of the Oscar-winning movie starring Jack Nicholson. Open from noon to 4pm Thursday to Saturday.

MAP: 4 P150 C3

city's Riverfront Park, formerly an industrial area with timber mills. Family-focused highlights of the 23-acre expanse now include a carousel and the **Gilbert House Children's Museum** *(acgilbert.org; admission $16)*. Closed on Mondays.

Named after AC Gilbert, the Salem-born toy inventor and manufacturer, the museum is crammed with interactive kid-friendly installations and includes examples of Gilbert's beloved playtime creations, including Erector sets and American Flyer trains.

Biking and walking trails – including a pedestrian bridge over the Willamette River – course through the park. Seek out the Eco-Earth Globe, a recycled piece of industrial waste that's been reinvented as a symbol of global peace with more than 86,000 colorful mosaic tiles.

Time Travel at the Willamette Heritage Center

HERITAGE PRECINCT

MAP: 5 P150 C3

Traveling history buffs should definitely explore this interesting 5-acre complex *(willametteheritage.org; adult/child $10/6)* combining leafy gardens with pioneer buildings and two museums. The Mission Mill Museum, Jason Lee House (1841), John Boon House (1847), the Methodist Parsonage (1841) and an old Presbyterian church (1858) all still authentically reflect their 1840s and 1850s origins.

Built in 1889, the Thomas Kay Woolen Mill was powered by a mill race (waterway), a section of which still runs through the grounds. Also showcased are the history and culture of the region's Indigenous Kalapuya people and the stories of pioneers making the arduous trek west on the Oregon Trail. Open Wednesday to Saturday.

Enjoy the Enchanted Forest

FAMILY FUN PARK

MAP: 6 P150 **C4**

Welcome to a family-friendly destination that's perfect for the longer days of summer. Located around 7 miles south of Salem, the **Enchanted Forest** *(enchantedforest.com; adult/child $29/26)* includes exciting highlights such as the Big Timber Log Ride and the Ice Mountain Bobsled Roller Coaster. Walk-through attractions include Storybook Lane – packed with characters from fairy tales and nursery rhymes – a heritage Western town and a European-style village. Spectacular fountains and light shows enliven proceedings after dark, and during summer, performers at the park's comedy theater ensure there are plenty of laughs. Opening dates and hours vary, but the park is generally open from late May to late September. Book online for good discounts on admission fees.

ELSINORE THEATRE

A dazzling Tudor-Gothic landmark in downtown Salem, **Elsinore Theatre** *(elsinoretheatre.com)* opened in 1926. It once showed silent movies, but is now primarily a venue for comedy and concerts. The 1778-pipe Wurlitzer organ is one of the nation's finest, and past performers include Hollywood legends Gregory Peck and James Earl Jones. Following stints working at a Silverton sawmill, Clark Gable used to practice his lines on the theater's stage. See the website for what's scheduled.

MAP: 8 P150 **B2**

Ride on Albany's Historic Carousel

HERITAGE TREASURE

MAP: 7 P150 **C4**

From Salem, detour 25 miles south to Albany, known for its heritage downtown precinct, but also the location of one of the nation's most loved carousels. Originally built in 1909, the **carousel** *(albanycarousel.com; ride $2)*, after stints in New Jersey and Pennsylvania, made its way via Santa Barbara to Albany, where it was restored across 10 years before reopening in 2017. All of the animals on the carousel – from greyhounds and frogs to Chinook salmon and honey bears – were carved by local volunteer artisans, and it's a work in progress with new ride-on creatures being added on an occasional basis. After a thrilling, memory-packed whirl on the carousel, look around the museum, and maybe check out what new menagerie additions are currently being worked on. Open from 11am to 4pm from Wednesday to Sunday.

LISTINGS

Best Places for...

See p150 for map of locations

$ Budget $$ Midrange $$$ Top End

Eating

Food Carts

Yard Food Park $

9

Four miles east of downtown Salem, Yard Food Park has 20 food carts serving up barbecue, sushi, burgers and pizza. There are also lots of fine Oregon craft beers. *theyardfoodpark.com; 11am-8pm Sun-Thu, to 9pm Fri & Sat*

Coffee & Breakfast

Margin Coffee Roasters $

10

Refuel in Albany's historic downtown precinct with excellent coffee and road-trip-worthy snacks, including bagels, quiche and cinnamon rolls. *margincoffee.com; 6:30am-5pm Mon-Fri, from 8am Sat & Sun*

Word of Mouth Bistro $$

This longstanding favorite of Salem locals serves superior spins on brunch classics. Look forward to tasty variations on French toast, eggs Benedict and hash browns. *wordofsalem.com; 6:45am-2pm Wed-Mon*

Relaxed Dining

Wild Pear $$

Loyal Salem regulars crowd in for soup, salads and sandwiches. There's a French bistro vibe and local art hung on the brick walls. *wildpearcatering.com; 10:30am-3:30pm Mon-Wed, to 6:30pm Thu, to 8pm Fri & Sat*

Cozy Taberna $$

Spanish-style dining with a good range of tapas-style plates made for sharing and hearty steak, chicken and seafood dishes. Popular weekend brunches include bloody Mary and mimosa cocktails. *thecozytaberna.com; 3-9pm Mon-Fri, 10am-9pm Sat & Sun*

Epilogue Kitchen & Cocktails $$

Detour 4 miles south of downtown to this easy-going combo of bistro and bar. Order from a pan-global menu or book in advance for three- and seven-course tasting menus from Thursday to Saturday. Occasional live music on Saturday nights. *epilogue-kitchen.square.site; 5-9pm Thu-Mon*

Fin+Fowl Kitchen $$

15

After hiking at Silver Falls State Park, stop in downtown Silverton for good-value Japanese-inspired bento bowls, poke and ramen. Ingredients are sourced from local farms. *finfowlkitchen.com; 11am-4:30pm*

Drinking

Craft Beer

Santiam Brewing

16

British-style brews flow at this well-established Salem brewery. Try the easy-drinking Spitfire Amber pale ale with a delicious Scotch egg. Nearby are several other taprooms making up Salem's unofficial brewery district. *santiam brewing.com; 11am-9pm*

Silver Falls Brewery

17

Fire pits and a summer – and dog-friendly patio make this Silverton taproom a popular year-round destination. Standout beers include the Double Falls IPA and the Oregon Sunshine Hazy IPA. Good pub food, too. *silverfallsbrewery. com; noon-8pm Wed-Mon*

Wine

Willamette Valley Vineyards

Situated on an imposing hilltop south of Salem, Willamette Valley Vineyards is one of Oregon's most respected wine producers. Book online for tasting-room and food-pairing experiences. The pinot noir is superb. *wvv.com; 11am-6pm Sat-Thu, to 8pm Fri*

Shopping

Gifts, Crafts & Souvenirs

The Reed

Sprawling shopping labyrinth housed in Salem's former Reed Opera House, and now accommodating everything from boutiques and vintage shops to pop-up jewelry and craft markets. *thereedsalem.com; 7am-10pm Mon-Sat, from 9am Sun*

Made in Oregon

In Salem with edible Oregon-sourced products, including cheese, wine, preserves and confectionery, along with gifts, souvenirs and arts and crafts. *madeinoregon. com; 11am-7pm Mon-Thu, 10am-8pm Fri & Sat, 11am-6pm Sun*

★ WORTH A TRIP

Visiting Mt Angel

Northeast of Salem, Mt Angel's European ambience comes from the arrival of Swiss Benedictine monks and Bavarian settlers in the late 19th-century. Easily combined with a visit to the Oregon Garden, the town is a fascinating slice of old-world Europe in the Oregon countryside.

GETTING THERE
From Salem to Mt Angel is around 18 miles. Bus 20X departs from Salem's Downtown Transit Center. Having your own vehicle allows a visit to the Oregon Garden en route.

Scan this QR code for info on Mount Angel Abbey and Benedictine Brewery.

Beer & Bavarian Heritage

From **Mt Angel** *(discovermtangel.org)* main street, which is dotted with Bavarian-style storefronts, make the short walk uphill to **St Mary Catholic Church**. Consecrated in 1910, this church features a beautiful nave and colorful murals. The left-hand door is usually unlocked for access. En route on Charles St, stop at the Bavarian-style **maibaum**, a blue-and-white-striped maypole depicting the trades of the residents who call Mt Angel home.

The town's annual **Mt Angel Oktoberfest** *(oktoberfest.org)* – the biggest in the Pacific Northwest – attracts revelers in September for four days of dancing, yodeling and plenty of beer and sausages. Many events are free, and Oregon's best breweries craft special German-style beers for the event.

Cloistered Quietude

On the forested edge of town, **Mount Angel Abbey** *(mountangelabbey.org)* is a Benedictine monastery featuring a theological library designed by Modernist architect Alvar Aalto, a bookshop and cafe, and a quirky museum crammed with idiosyncratic taxidermy.

GINA KELLY/ALAMY

See the abbey's website for a self-guided 14-stop walking tour around the leafy grounds, and enjoy Belgian-style abbey beers brewed by the monks at the adjacent **Benedictine Brewery** (*benedictinebrewery.com*; pictured). Both the St Benedict farmhouse ale and the St Gabriel Belgian *dubbel* are divine brews. The abbey and the brewery are both closed on Monday and Tuesday.

QUICK BREAK
Hearty servings of German-style pretzels, sausages and schnitzel all partner with lashings of Bavarian lager and *hefeweizen* (wheat beer) at the **Mt Angel Sausage Company**. *Prost!*

Portland Toolkit

Family Travel 162

Accommodations 163

Food, Drink & Nightlife 164

LGBTIQ+ Travel 166

Health & Safe Travel 167

Responsible Travel 168

Accessible Travel 170

Nuts & Bolts 171

Steel Bridge

BRAM REUSEN/SHUTTERSTOCK

Family Travel

Ease of public transport, a compact cityscape and a wide range of kid-friendly activities make Portland a good option for traveling families. Attractions around the Willamette Valley include family-friendly trails to spectacular waterfalls.

Is Portland Good for Kids?

With one of the country's lowest birth rates, Portland is actually not an overly child-focused city, but there is still plenty to see and do as a family. Strollers are welcome on the MAX Light Rail service, and if Pacific Northwest rain sets in, escape to the planet's largest independent bookstore.

PLAYGROUNDS & MORE

One of the most popular playgrounds is Rose Garden Children's Playground in **Washington Park**. Other kid-friendly locations in Portland include **Hopscotch** and **OMSI**.

Scan the QR code to discover the Portland area's best playgrounds.

Eating Out

Children's menus are not widely available. Exceptions include chain restaurants, and some craft-brewery taprooms where quizzes and crayons might be given to younger patrons while mom and dad are enjoying a seasonal brew. **Deschutes Brewery Portland Public House** even has a play area. With lots of different cuisines, food cart pods are a good option for fussy diners.

Breastfeeding

Breastfeeding in public is protected under Oregon state law. Some restaurants, especially if chain-run, offer parenting rooms with change tables.

Public Transport

Children six and under travel free and those between seven and 17 pay a reduced fare.

Admission Fees

Oregon Zoo (p57), **Portland Art Museum** (p46), the **Oregon Historical Society Museum** (p25) and the **Chinatown Museum** (p68) reduce admission for kids. The **Portland Puppet Museum** (p36) is free for all.

FROM LEFT; XPIXEL/SHUTTERSTOCK, STEFAN FOTO VIDEO/SHUTTERSTOCK

Accommodations

Hip boutique rooms, revived historic hotels and wine-country B&Bs are options in Portland and the Willamette Valley.

Where to Stay if You Love...

A Convenient Central Cocation

Downtown (p41) Good public-transport links and airport access, with after-dark attractions like performing-arts centers and top-end restaurants. Portland's central hub for luxury and chain hotels.

Art, Shopping, Eating & Drinking

Northeast (p89) Hip bars, restaurants and breweries, quirky retailers, and the Alberta Arts District. Accommodation includes heritage buildings and an urban spa experience at Cascada.

We love to stay in...

The Northwest & Pearl District (p73)

On downtown's northern edge, the restaurants, cafes and shops of the Pearl's revitalized warehouse district adjoins Nob Hill and the tree-lined leisure thoroughfare of NW 23rd Ave. Nearby, formerly industrial Slabtown hosts innovative craft breweries and good-value hotels.

An Eclectic Urban Vibe

Southeast (p103) Great eating and drinking with restaurants, food carts and brewery taprooms. Also live music and surprising shopping. Recently renovated historic hotels and stylish boutique stays.

A Historic Downtown

McMinnville (p127) Stay in boutique hotels in the town's heritage downtown precinct. Good eateries and vineyard tasting rooms. A short drive to a brilliant aviation museum.

Rural Ambience

Newberg & Dundee (p139) High-end spa hotels and welcoming inns and B&Bs in the heart of Willamette Valley wine country. Highly regarded restaurants and an interesting craft-beer scene.

HOW MUCH FOR A NIGHT IN

Hostel dorm bed **from $70**

Midrange hotel **from $135**

Top-end downtown hotel **from $250**

Food, Drink & Nightlife

Allergies & Intolerances

Beyond national chain restaurants, there is no Oregon state requirement for menus to list ingredients, but it's commonplace - and increasingly smart business practice - for hospitality operators to provide this for the city's significant number of diners requesting gluten-free, keto or vegan options. Many cafes and restaurants provide the option to substitute gluten-free ingredients for a small premium.

FOOD CARTS

Food carts are popular throughout Portland and in Willamette Valley towns. Look forward to flavors from around the world, and also dishes from younger chefs getting a start in the business.

THE CASE FOR CASH

The option of contactless payment is now almost ubiquitous, but cash is handy at farmers markets or when buying produce from farm stands during summer.

SUMMERTIME SNACKING

Beyond the Willamette Valley's focus on growing grapes and hops, other local crops are also harvested across summer. Negotiate rural backroads to seek out orchard-fresh cherries and strawberries from June, and ask at local cafes and bakeries if freshly baked marionberry cobbler is on the menu.

Restaurant Reservations

Resy, OpenTable and Tock are the main online platforms for restaurant reservations, and increasingly, a credit card is needed to guarantee the booking. For weekend brunches, especially at the city's most popular cafes, you may need to queue before securing a table.

HOW TO... Pay the Bill

For cafes and food carts, it's normal to pay at the counter when you order. At restaurants, signal to waitstaff that you're ready to pay.

Splitting the bill: If you require split bills, mention this when ordering to avoid any confusion. Consider using the Splitwise app to keep track of payments when traveling in a group.

Tipping: A tip of 20% is standard for restaurant dining, while 15% is acceptable for takeout occasions like coffee or a food cart. Screens for contactless payments show a range of options, usually beginning at 15% to 18%. Adding cash to tip jars at cafes and food carts is also an option.

PRICE RANGES

The following price ranges refer to the cost of an average main course.

$ less than $15
$$ $15–25
$$$ more than $25

OPENING HOURS

Cafes 7am to 3pm
Craft-brewery taprooms noon to 10pm
Restaurants 11:30 to 2pm and 5pm to 9pm. Often closed between lunch and dinner

Going Out

Craft breweries Brewery taprooms are not a late-night scene, with most venues both family- and dog-friendly. Weekend afternoons plus spring and summer evenings are popular times to visit. Cider and craft-distilled spirits are also growing in importance.

Bars & clubs Portland doesn't have a big clubbing scene and locals are just as likely to enjoy craft cocktails or an Eastside gig. Popular venues include **Holocene** and the **White Owl Social Club**. See **doPDX** *(dopdx.com)* for events.

Vineyard tasting rooms Willamette Valley vineyards do feature on-site tasting rooms, but also have downtown locations in McMinnville, Newberg and Dundee. There's often a tasting fee refundable with a purchase of wine. Weekends, especially in warmer seasons, are busy, so consider a weekday visit. Check opening hours before departing. Some venues require prior booking.

PROSTOCK-STUDIO/SHUTTERSTOCK

HOW MUCH FOR A

Coffee
$5

Cinnamon scroll
$6

Diner breakfast
$20

Food cart taco
$5

Craft beer
$7

Taproom burger
$20

Restaurant main course
$35

Artisan ice cream
$10

LGBTIQ+ Travelers

This is an LGBTIQ+-friendly destination where queer culture is ingrained in the social fabric of a proudly inclusive community.

LGBTIQ+

Portland has one of the highest populations of LGBTIQ+ residents in the country. Rainbow flags enliven houses in residential neighborhoods and feature in the windows of shops and businesses. There is no specific 'gayborhood' in the city, but the Old Town and Chinatown area has gay venues, including the male-strip-club vibe of **Silverado**. On the city's Eastside are **Back2Earth** and **Eagle Portland**.

LGBTIQ+ politicians to make their mark in Portland and the Willamette Valley include Kate Brown, Oregon's governor from 2015 to 2023; Tina Kotek, the state's incumbent governor from 2023; and winemaker Remy Drabkin, mayor of McMinnville from 2022 to 2024.

Darcelle XV Showcase

Named after Walter Willard Cole – aka Darcelle – this Old Town **nightlife spot** has been a Portland institution since 1967. When aged almost 86, Darcelle was certified by Guinness World Records as the world's oldest drag performer in 2016, and following her death in 2023, the club remains a popular drag venue.

PORTLAND PRIDE

July's **Portland Pride** *(portlandpride.org)* includes Oregon's largest parade – drawing thousands plus the Dykes on Bikes to downtown Portland – and an inclusive Waterfront Festival.

QUEER WINE FEST

Late June's annual **Queer Wine Fest** is held at Remy Wines near the Willamette Valley town of Dayton. **Scan the QR code for details.**

Resources

- **Q Center** *(pdxqcenter.org)* Supporting Portland's LGBTIQ+ community.
- **PDX Queer Meetup** *@pdxqueermeetup* on Instagram and promoting regular events around the city.
- **Queer Social Club** *(queersocialclub.com)* Listings could include Sapphic speed dating and Loud & Queer open-mic nights at craft breweries.

FROM LEFT: CHERYL JUETTEN, NITO/SHUTTERSTOCK

Health & Safe Travel

Despite the odd headline about public demonstrations and the homeless population, Portland is a safe city for travelers to visit.

PROTESTS IN PORTLAND

In 2020, more than 100 consecutive days of protest in support of the BLM movement occurred in Portland. Significant protests during the first 100 days of the Trump administration in 2025 also took place, but were peaceful and posed no problems for visitors.

Homelessness in Portland

Homelessness in Portland is a significant and visible issue, especially around the Old Town area. Largely the city's homeless population pose minimal danger to visitors, but avoiding certain areas after dark is recommended. If you do notice somebody experiencing behavioral issues, contact the trained non-police responder team at **Portland Street Response** *(portlandstreetresponse.org)*. Buying the Street Roots *(streetroots.org)* newspaper provides support to the city's homeless community.

Tap Water

Safe to drink and restaurants will serve you complimentary water when you sit down.

Insurance

The cost of healthcare in the US is very expensive, and it's therefore imperative to have your own travel and medical insurance. If you're renting a vehicle, it's also worth including Supplemental Liability Insurance (SLI) to protect yourself in the case of financial responsibility for injury or property damage caused to others while driving.

HIKING SAFETY PROTOCOL

Always hike with a buddy in the Columbia Gorge and Silver Falls State Park, and share your hiking plans before departure.

QUICK INFO

Security

Don't leave valuables visible in your vehicle. Break-ins are a common problem.

Cannabis

Legal to purchase and use for ages 21 and over. Don't light up in public spaces.

DUI

Driving under the influence applies to both alcohol and drugs.

Responsible Travel

Follow these tips to leave a lighter footprint, support local and have a positive impact on communities.

Cycling

With around 400 miles of bikeways, greenways and other multi-use paths through most residential neighborhoods, Portland is often named the most bike-friendly city in the US. More than one thousand electric-assisted bikes are available throughout the city's app-based **Biketown** *(biketownpdx.com)* service. E-scooters are available from Biketown and via the Lime app. Biketown bikes and E-scooters can't be taken on public transport.

Don't Forget to Bus...

At cafes and food carts, it's usually expected diners will 'bus' (return their empty plates) to a common location. Receptacles are provided to separate food waste and recyclable items.

FROM LEFT: NAME/CREDIT, NAME/CREDIT, NAME/CREDIT

OUR PICK

Astera

At **Astera** farmed and foraged ingredients from around the Pacific Northwest feature on sustainable and plant-based tasting menus of up to 10 courses.

Bring Your Own Bag

Single-use plastic bags were banned in Portland in 2020. Paper bags and multi-use plastic bags are sold cheaply by supermarkets, but having your own tote bags for shops and farmers markets is a more sustainable option. Portland's most popular markets are Saturday morning's **Portland Farmers Market at PSU** and the Wednesday market in Shemanski Park at **South Park Blocks**.

Resources

• **shopsmallpdx.com** Over 1700 local shops, eateries and services. • **mercatus.pdx** BIPOC-owned businesses, including the city's only Native American-owned coffeehouse.

FROM LEFT: ALEXANDER OGANEZOV/SHUTTERSTOCK, IVICA DRUSANY/SHUTTERSTOCK, SELIN AYDOGAN/SHUTTERSTOCK

SUSTAINABLE PDX

The recent redevelopment of **Portland International Airport** (PDX) includes features such as a spectacular roof made of locally grown, sustainably harvested wood, and an ongoing program to accelerate the use of sustainable aviation fuel.

Vintage Shopping

Browsing for vintage clothing is a popular pastime in Portland, and the city is renowned for its range of retro retailers. Southeast Portland, especially around the Hawthorne neighborhood, is the epicenter of a vintage scene that attracts Hollywood stars and Pacific Northwest music royalty.

Telephone Vintage in Hawthorne has hats and T-shirts aplenty, while west along SE Hawthorne Blvd, **Magpie** is always worth a browse. To the northwest, **Yellowstone Vintage** features everything from 1940s ski parkas to very collectable 1980s grunge-era T-shirts, but also more affordable posters and accessories.

IN THE WILLAMETTE VALLEY

There are farmers markets and seasonal farm stands around the Willamette Valley. Be sure to bring along some cash.

Scan the QR code for details.

Climate Change & Travel

It's impossible to ignore the impact we have when traveling; Lonely Planet urges all travelers to engage with their travel carbon footprint, which will mainly come from air travel. While there often isn't an alternative, travelers can look to minimize the number of flights they take, opt for newer aircrafts and use cleaner ground transport, such as trains. One proposed solution—purchasing carbon offsets—unfortunately does not cancel out the impact of individual flights. While most destinations will depend on air travel for the foreseeable future, for now, pursuing ground-based travel where possible is the best course of action.

The **UN Carbon Offset Calculator** shows how flying impacts a household's emissions

The **ICAO's carbon emissions calculator** allows visitors to analyse the CO2 generated by point-to-point journeys

Accessible Travel

Public Transport

Portland's public transport system, Trimet, includes ramps on buses, streetcars and MAX Light Rail services, and station lifts with priority seating available on all transport. Textured floor tiles and Braille/raised-letter signage supports blind/reduced vision travelers. Search 'Accessibility' on *trimet.org*.

At the Airport

Portland International Airport (PDX) is known for being welcoming and accessible. 'Hidden disability' sunflower lanyards are available. Counter hearing loop systems provide assistive listening technology, and trained therapy dogs can ease airport anxiety.

OUR PICK

Portland Art Museum (p46) offers support for travelers with accessibility needs. This includes wheelchair and mobility scooter access to all galleries, audio guides via the Bloomberg Connect app, and EnChroma glasses for visitors with color blindness. Magnifying devices and iPads are available to assist visitors with reduced vision, and the Sensing Art exhibition features tactile raised-line artworks for blind or low-vision visitors. Curb cuts also feature at car parks and entrances.

ADAPTIVE CYCLING

To increase access to cycling in this bike-crazy city, **Adaptive BIKETOWN** *(adaptivebiketown.com)* rents hand- and foot-powered recumbent bikes. Electric-assisted options are available, along with an e-assisted Trio Taxi multi-person bike.

Ride-Sharing

Uber offers wheelchair-accessible rides through its Uber WAV service, with drivers trained to assist mobility-challenged passengers. Choose WAV under vehicle options. For Lyft, add 'Wheelchair Access' under Settings.

NEGOTIATING THE CITY

Crosswalks around the city offer audio notifications, and sidewalks around downtown have curb cuts for wheeled access. Pedestrian- and bike-friendly paths along Naito Pwy are also suitable for wheelchairs.

Resources

• **travelportland.com** Search 'Accessible Portland' for information. • **wheeltheworld.com** Search 'Portland'. Includes a list of accessible hotels and restaurants.

Nuts & Bolts

Opening Hours

The following opening hours are a general guide. Check individual listings and businesses for specifics.

Diners & cafes 7am–3pm

Restaurants lunch 11:30am–2pm, dinner 5–9pm

Food carts 11am–9pm, some only open for dinner

Brewpubs noon–10pm

Supermarkets 7am–10pm (sometimes 24hr)

Shops 9am–5pm (malls to 9pm); sometimes also open on weekends

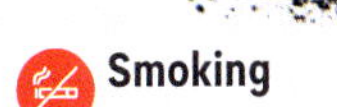

QUICK INFO

Time zone
Pacific Standard Time (GMT/UTC minus seven/eight hours)

City code
+503 and +971

Emergency number
911

Population
630,500

ELECTRICITY

120V/60Hz

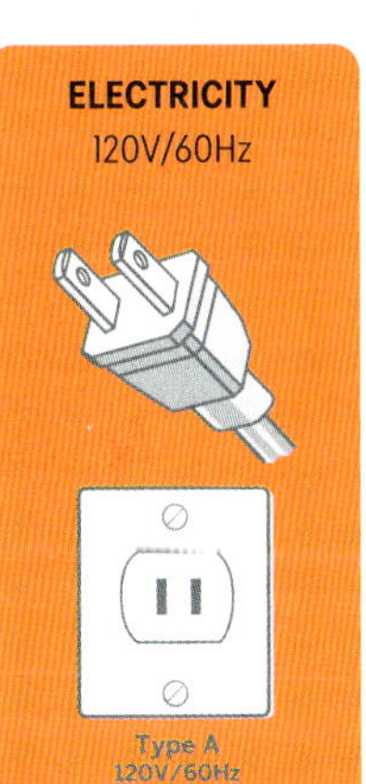

Public Holidays

New Year's Day 1 January

Martin Luther King Jr Day Third Monday of January

President's Day Third Monday of February

Memorial Day Third Monday of May

Juneteenth (commemorating the end of slavery in the US) 19 June

Independence Day 4 July

Labor Day First Monday of September

Veteran's Day 11 November

Thanksgiving Fourth Thursday of November

Day after Thanksgiving Fourth Friday of November

Christmas Day 25 December

Smoking

Oregon's Indoor Clean Air Act (2007) prohibits smoking and using e-cigarettes in all public buildings, shops, bars and restaurants. City ordinance also prohibits smoking at designated city parks, trails and open spaces, and within 20ft of city-owned or city-maintained playgrounds, beaches and athletic facilities.

FROM LEFT: VALZAN/SHUTTERSTOCK, MADERLA/SHUTTERSTOCK

Index

Sights p000 Map pages **p000**

See also separate subindexes for:
Eating p174
Drinking p175
Shopping p175

accessible travel 170
accommodations 163
activities 22, 30
- Evergreen Wings & Waves Waterpark 135
- Experience Oregon 46
- Hopscotch Portland 110
- Oregon Zoo 57
- Portland Spirit 48

Albany's Historic Carousel 155
Alberta Arts District 97
arriving 32

B

bicycles & e-scooters **168**

C

car rentals 33
Cascada Thermal Springs + Hotel 95, 96
city code 171
climate 30, 169
Columbia River Gorge, The 116
costs 34
cycling 168

disabilities, travelers 170
Downtown & Southwest Portland 41-53, **42-3**, **49**
- eating 50-1
- experiences 46-8
- drinking 51-2
- itineraries 44-5, **44**
- shopping 52-3
- transportation 41
- walking tours 44-5, **44**

drinking 14, 137, 164, *see also individual neighborhoods,* Drinking *subindex*
Dundee, *see* Newberg & Dundee

eating 12, 112, 136, 164, *see also individual neighborhoods,* Eating *subindex*
electricity 171
emergency numbers 171
entertainment 18
- 99W Drive-In 144
- Alberta Rose Theatre 95
- Avalon Theatre 109
- Cameo 144
- Cinema 21 83
- CoHo Theatre 83
- Darcelle XV Showplace 69
- Elsinore Theatre 155
- Funland Entertainment Center 122
- Hollywood Theatre 96
- McMenamins Mission Theater 83
- Portland Center Stage at the Armory 83

events & festivals 30
- Cherry Blossom Day 153
- Christmas tree-lighting ceremony 46
- Dragon Dance Parade 68
- International Pinot Noir Festival 134
- Mt Angel Oktoberfest 30, 158
- Portland Adult Soapbox Derby 31, 111
- Portland Pride Waterfront Festival 30, 47
- Portland Rose Festival City Fair 47
- Queer Wine Fest 134
- UFO Fest 134
- Waterfront Blues Festival 47

F

family travel 23, 162
festivals, *see* festivals & events
food 12, 112, 136, 164, *see also individual neighborhoods,* Eating *subindex*

galleries & museums 20
- Artemis Fox Gallery 135
- Blackfish Gallery 81
- Blue Sky, Oregon Center for the Photographic Arts 81
- Confederated Tribes of Grand Ronde Center for Native American Art 46
- Confederated Tribes of the Grand Ronde Gallery 153
- Currents Gallery 135
- Elizabeth Leach Gallery 81
- Evergreen Aviation & Space Museum 134
- First Thursday Street Gallery 81
- Freakybuttrue Peculiarium 82
- Gallery 114 81
- Gilbert House Children's Museum 154
- Guardino Gallery 95
- Hallie Ford Museum of Art 153
- Hoover-Minthorn House 143
- ILY2 81
- J Pepin Art Gallery 81
- Japanese American Museum of Oregon 67, 68
- John Stromme Art Gallery 135
- OMSI (Oregon Museum of Science & Industry) 106
- Oregon Film Museum 120
- Oregon Historical Society Museum 46
- Oregon Maritime Museum 47

OSH Museum of Mental Health 154
Portland Art Museum 46
Portland Chinatown Museum 67, 68
Portland Puppet Museum 111
World Forestry Center Discovery Museum 57
gardens 19
Crystal Springs Rhododendron Garden 110
International Rose Test Garden 54
Lan Su Chinese Garden 67
Portland Japanese Garden 54
Oregon Garden, The 151
gay & lesbian travelers 21, 166

H

health 167
highlights 6-23, 62-3, 64-5, 76-7, 78-9, 92-3, 106-7, 116-9, 120-5, 128-9, 141, 146, 151, 152, 158-9
hiking safety 167
homelessness 167
Hood River 119

I

itineraries 24, *see also individual neighborhoods*

J

Japanese American Historical Plaza 67-8

Lan Su Chinese Garden 64, 67
LGBTIQ+ travelers 21, 166
literary experiences 8

McMenamins Kennedy School 92
McMinnville 127-137, **128**
drinking 137
eating 136-7
experiences 129-31, 134-5
itineraries 132-3, **132**
shopping 137
transportation 127
walking tours 132-3, **132**
museums. *see* galleries & museums
Mt Angel 158
Mt Tabor 110
Multnomah Village 48, 49

Newberg & Dundee 139-145, **140**
drinking 145
eating 145
experiences 141-4
shopping 145
transportation 139
nightlife 164, *see also* entertainment
Northeast & North Portland 89-101, **90-1**
drinking 100
eating 98-100
experiences 92-3, 96-7
itineraries 94-5, **94**
shopping 101
transportation 89
walking tours 94-5, **94**
Northwest Portland & Pearl District 73-87, **74-5**
drinking 86-7
eating 85-6
experiences 76-9, 82-4
itineraries 80-1, **80**
shopping 87
transportation 73
walking tours 80-1, **80**

Old Town Chinatown 59-71, **60-1**
drinking 71
eating 70-1
experiences 62-5, 68-9
itineraries 66-7, **66**
shopping 71
transportation 59
walking tours 66-7, **66**
OMSI (Oregon Museum of Science & Industry) 106
opening hours 171
Oregon City 146
Oregon Coast, The 120
Oregon Garden, The 151
Oregon State Capitol 153

parks
Fort Stevens State Park 120
Governor Tom McCall Waterfront Park 45, 46
Laurelhurst Park 109, 110
Mill Ends Park 45, 47
Mt Tabor Park 110
Peninsula Park 96
Riverfront Park 153
Silver Falls State Park 152
South Park Blocks 45
Washington Park 54
Pearl District, *see* Northwest Portland & Pearl District
Pioneer Courthouse Square 45-6
population 171
Portland Aerial Tram 48
Portland Building 45
Portland Horse Project 36
Portland Pride Waterfront Festival 30, 47
Portland Saturday Market 62, 67
Portland Visitor Center 45
Powell's City of Books 76
protests 167
public holidays 171
public transportation 33

responsible travel 168
rideshare & taxis 33

safe travel 167
Salem 149-157, **150**
drinking 157
eating 156
experiences 151-5
shopping 157
transportation 149
shopping 16, 137 *see also individual neighborhoods,* Shopping *subindex*
Silver Falls State Park 152
smoking 171

Southeast
Portland 103-115, **104-5**
drinking 114-5
eating 112-4
experiences 106-7, 110-1
itineraries 108-9, **108**
shopping 115
transportation 103
walking tours 108-9, **108**
Southwest Portland, *see* Downtown & Southwest Portland
surprises 36

tap water 167
taxis 33
time zones 171
transportation 32, 33, *see also individual neighborhoods*
travel seasons 30
traveling with kids 162

Washington Park 54-7, 56
waterfalls
Fairy Falls 117
Horsetail Falls 118
Latourell Falls 117
Multnomah Falls 116
Silver Falls State Park 152
Upper Oneonta Falls 118
Wahclella Falls 119
Wahkeena Falls 117
Willamette Falls 147
weather 30-1, 169
wellness experiences 6
Willamette Heritage Center 154
Wine Spa 96
wine tasting 10, 84
Adelsheim Vineyard 141
Ambar Estate 142
Chris James Cellars 130
Hood River Wineries 119
Ken Wright Cellars 130
Remy Wines 130, 134
Roco Winery 141
Soter Vineyards 142
Stoller Family Estate 130
Stoller Wine Bar 130
Willamette Valley Wine Touring 128
Wine Touring Around Newberg & Dundee 141

Eating

Abuela's Nuestra Cocina 136
Akadi 114
Al-Amir Restaurant 51
Andina 86
Astera 112
Baby Doll Pizza 113
BKK Pad Thai 113
Bole Ethiopian Restaurant 99
Cafe Rosetta 98
Café United 70
Camp 18 121
Chilango 99
Coffee Time 85
Cozy Taberna 156
Crescent Cafe 136
Daily Feast 50
Dan & Louis Oyster Bar 71
DarSalam Restaurant 99
DC Vegetarian 113
Departure 50
Dil Se 50
Dolly Olive 50
Dragonfly Coffee House 85
El Nutri Taco 99
Empirical Café 107
Enat Kitchen 99
Epilogue Kitchen & Cocktails 156
Escape from NY Pizza 86
Farmer and the Beast 85
Feral 100
Fin+Fowl Kitchen 156
Gado Gado 98
Gastro Mania Deli NW 85
Guilder Cafe 77
Hat Yai 98
Hayward 136
HiFi Wine Bar 136
Higgins 50
Horse Radish 136
Humble Spirit 136
Jade Rabbit 113
Jake's Famous Crawfish 51
Jam on Hawthorne 112
Joel Palmer House 137
John's Cafe 70
Kabba's Kitchen 114
Kachka 112
Kann 112
Kate's Ice Cream 99
Kati Portland 113
Kayo's Ramen Bar 98
Ken's Artisan Pizza 113
Kingsland Kitchen 70
Langbaan 85
Lechon 70
Luc Lac Vietnamese Kitchen 50
Mac Market 136
Mac Plaza 129
Mamma Khouri's 99
Margin Coffee Roasters 156
Maruti Indian Restaurant 113
Mediterranean Exploration Company 86
Mémoire Cà Phê 98
Mike's Drive In 147
Mirisata 113
Mississippi Pizza 99
Monte Rossa Cafe 70
Mother's Bistro 50
Mucca Osteria 51
Nepali Kitchen and Chai Garden 98
Normandie 112
Nostrana 112
Oven and Shaker 86
Painted Lady 145
Papa Haydn 85
Paradox Cafe 112
PDX Original Elephant Ears 63
Pine Street Market 70
Portland City Grill 50
Potato Champion 113
Proud Mary 99
Rabbits Cafe 51
Red Hills Market 144
Salt & Straw 95, 99
Serendipity Ice Cream 133
Sizzle Pie 100
Southpark Seafood 51
Storrs Smokehouse 145
Sushi Ichiban 70
Tahrir Square 113
Takibi 82

TapTap Cuisine 98
Thai Peacock 50
Thistle 133
Tina's 145
Tin Shed Garden Cafe 98
Top Burmese Burma Joy 85
Urdaneta 100
Village Kitchen 85
Voodoo Doughnut 67, 69
Walk the Wok 51
Wild Pear 156
Wilf's Restaurant & Jazz Bar 70
Word of Mouth Bistro 156
Xin Ding Dumpling House 70
Yaad Style Jamaican Cuisine 98
Yard Food Park 156

Drinking

45 East 114
Abigail Hall 51
Alchemist's Jam & Bakery 133
Back2Earth 100
Barley & Vine Tavern 145
Bauman's on Oak 114
Bible Club 114
Blue Moon Lounge 137
Boedecker Cellars 84
Breakside Brewery 86
Bull Run Distillery 137
Bye and Bye 100
Comala 87
Creepy's 114
Dante's 71
Daydream 115
Deschutes Brewery Portland Public House 86
Eagle Portland 100
Fools and Horses 86
ForeLand Beer 133
Fortune 51
Fossil & Fawn 84
Gibson 52
Green Room 51
Ground Kontrol Classic Arcade and Bar 68
Grove Tasting Room 133
Haven Coffee Co 79
Heater Allen Brewing 137
Holocene 114
Hopworks Urban Brewery 114
Hungry Tiger 114
Kell's Irish Pub 71
Kelly's Olympian 52
McMenamins Hotel Oregon 137
Multnomah Whiskey Library 52
Nectaris 115
Palomar 86
Pharmacy, The 86
Pope House Bourbon Lounge 87
Proper Pint Oakroom 52
Proud Mary 95
Rachel & Rose 52
Raven's Manor 71
Remy Wines 130
Root & Rye Hop Farm and Brewery 137
Rose & Thistle Public House 100
Rose City Book Pub 100
Roseland Theater 71
Santiam Brewing 157
Ship Tavern 52
Silverado 71
Silver Falls Brewery 157
Sousòl 114
Stumptown Taps 145
Tao of Tea 109
Teardrop Lounge 87
Umami Café 55
Victoria Bar 100
White Owl Social Club 115
Wilderton Aperitivo Co 117
Willamette Valley Vineyards 157
Wolves & People Farmhouse Brewery 144
Village Coffee 48

Shopping

Always Here Bookstore 101
Annie Bloom's 52
Broadway Books 101
Cargo 111
Cherries & Figs Wine Shop 101
Communion 115
Crafty Wonderland 53
Ecovibe 101
Frances May 52
Friends Library Store 53
Frock Boutique 101
Gifty Kitty 101
Gold Door Jewelry & Arts 109
Goodies Snack Shop 71
Grand Gesture 53
Hello from Portland 87
Hip Hound 82
Indigo Traders 53
Ipnosi 82
John's Marketplace 48
JP General 53
Kiriko Made 52
Literary Arts Bookstore 115
Made in Oregon 157
MadeHere 87
Magpie 115
Meadow, The 87
Monograph Bookwerks 95
Mother Foucault's Bookshop 115
MudPuddles Toys & Books 82
New Renaissance Bookstore 82
NW Food and Gifts 133
Oblation Papers & Press 87
Ora et Labora 101
Paper Source 87
Paxton Gate 101
Peggy Sundays 53
Porch Light 87
Powell's Books on Hawthorne 109
Presents of Mind 109
Red Hills Market 145
Reed, The 157
SaySay Boutique 52
Snow Peak 82
Telephone Vintage 115
Third Street Books 133
Tumbleweed 101
Twill Boutique 115
Velour 145
Verdun Chocolates 87
Vintage on Third 137
Vortex 137
Way of Being 109
Yellowstone Vintage 115
Thinker Toys 48

Send Us Your Feedback

We love to hear from travellers – your comments help make our books better. We read every word, and we guarantee that your feedback goes straight to the authors. Visit lonelyplanet.com/contact to submit your updates and suggestions.

Note: We may edit, reproduce and incorporate your comments in Lonely Planet products such as guidebooks, websites and digital products, so let us know if you are happy to have your name acknowledged. For a copy of our privacy policy visit lonelyplanet.com/legal.

Acknowledgements

Cover photograph: Waterfront Park with Hawthorne Bridge on the Willamette River, Portland, Oregon.
ARTYOORAN/Shutterstock

Back photograph: Silver Falls, Willamette Valley, Oregon.
Michael Warwick/Shutterstock

THIS BOOK

The 3rd edition of Lonely Planet's Portland & the Willamette Valley guidebook was researched and written by Margot Bigg and Brett Atkinson. The previous edition was written by Celeste Brash. This guidebook was produced by the following:

Destination Editor
Melissa Yeager

Cartographer
Vojtech Bartos

Production Editor
Lucy Jones

Image Editor
Norma Brewer

Coordinating Editor
Simon Williamson

Cover Researcher
Giada de Agostinis

Thanks to
Ronan Abayawickrema, Janet Austin, Imogen Bannister, Kat Rowan

Published by Lonely Planet Global Limited
CRN 554153
3rd edition – Jan 2026
ISBN 9781837584192

10 9 8 7 6 5 4 3 2 1
Printed in Malaysia